UNIVERSAL SCIENCE-RELIGION

PHILOSOPHY OF HINDUISM
An Introduction
By T. C. Galav

"I owed a magnificent day to the Bhagvadgita. It was as if an empire spoke to us, nothing small or unworthy, but large serene, consistent, the voice of an old intelligence which in another age and climate had pondered and thus disposed of the same questions which exercise us."

Ralph Waldo Emerson

ACKNOWLEDGEMENTS:

The author gratefully acknowledges certain quotations which have not been formally mentioned.

And special thanks are expressed to Mrs. Galav For her continued inspiration, total help and support in the arduous task of finishing this book single handedly.

Second Edition: 1999

Printed in the United States of America
By John S. Swift Company, New Jersey, U.S.A.

Price: $12.00

TABLE OF CONTENTS

	PREFACE	I
Chptr. I	The Hindu Aryans	1
Chptr. II	Hindu Contributions	13
Chptr. III	Hinduism - Its Sources	23
Chptr. IV	The Guides In Hindu Literature	31
Chptr. V	The Goal	37
Chptr. VI	The Lower Goals (God and Goddesses)	41
Chptr. VII	Work and Worship	45
Chptr. VIIII	Paramatma, Brahman (God or Whatever)	51
Chptr. IX	Summary of Hindu Metaphysics (Shrimad Bhagvadgita)	67
Chptr. X	The Yogas - The Four Great Paths of Bhagvadgita	77
Chptr. XI	Lord God Krishna In The Gita	83
Chptr. XII	Transmigration of Soul	87
Chptr. XIII	Material Nature	93
Chptr. XIV	Karma Yoga	99
Chptr. XV	Raja Yoga	111
Chptr. XVI	Bhakti Yoga	119
Chptr. XVII	Nature's Eternal Religion	125

Chptr. XVIII	Rabindranath Tagore ....129 (1861 - 1941)	
Chptr. XIX	Swami Vivekananda ....133 (1863 - 1904)	
Chptr. XX	Aurobindo Ghose ....137 (1872 - 1950)	
Chptr. XXI	Mahatma Gandhi..........................141 (1869 - 1948)	
Chptr. XXII	Sarvepalli Radhakrishnan ....147 (1888 - 1975)	
Chptr. XXIII	The Epics 153	
Chptr. XXIV	The Story of Ramayana 159	
Chptr. XXV	The Story of Mahabharata 177	

* * * * *

PREFACE

It is presumptuous to write on the stupendous philosophy of Hinduism, which is a subject of Freedom, Right and Reason for the welfare of human race. Its focus is on the individual's behavior first; the society comes later because if the individual is good the society in which he lives is bound to be good and worth living for him and his family. To describe Hinduism is like describing the universal moral order which is what it is; and is nothing but a prescription for the right conduct for the individual and the society.

Freedom is the subject of this book as freedom (moksha) has been the burden of all the Hindu thought from Manu, Yagnavalkya, and Parashar to Veda Vyasa, Buddha, Sankara, Tulsidas, Nanak and Vivekananda of the modern period. This freedom is not political, religious or economic that the most Westerners have been obsessed with, but is what most Hindus aspire as the goal of their life in the same way as the great German philosopher Schopenhauer cried out to say in his uninhibited frenzy that "it has been the solace of my life, and it will be the solace of my death," or as the great French historian Jules Michelet said in his ecstasy that "... A serene peace reigns there; and in the midst of conflict an infinite sweetness, a boundless fraternity, which spreads over all living things, as ocean (without bottom or bound) of love, of pity, of clemency."

This freedom is a unique condition of the mind and the soul. It does not rest on the mundane freedoms though they may be helpful to certain categories of people and may not very much hurt the true goal seekers either. The people of all countries and climes have no doubt enjoyed this freedom, but the great minds of the West like Schopenhauer, Michelet, Thoreau and Emerson, among many others, made no secret of finding the real nectar in it. And history is the witness of not only the countless ordinary Hindu men and women who usually retired for the pursuit of this moksha, but also many a Hindu kings and public leaders who renounced their kingdoms (a rarity in the West) in pursuit of this goal only to weaken their country for repeated foreign invasions and wholesale destruction of their religion and the culture which they considered so precious.

The Hindus pursued the concept of freedom (moksha) to the point of their social regression and division of the society in castes and sub castes, each trying to be better than the other, usually repressing the weaker sections; and in mutual fighting of jealous kings and rajas encouraging outsiders to help one against the other until in the absence of a strong sovereign national government the whole India lay at the feet of and was subjugated by the shrewd rapacious conquerors. However, after regaining freedom as the Hindus have revived their glorious philosophies enshrined in the Upnishadas and the Bhagvadgita, this strife torn world which is still busy fighting religious wars, butchering innocent men and women, the children and the old for their fault of belonging to a different religion, may be able to hope to find a religion free philosophy for a peaceful coexistence. This is very much possible because in the name of religion, the Hindus have never used force to subjugate others or compel them to be proselytized to their ways by showing fear, force or favors.

The Hindu thought was glorified by Warren Hastings, the

conqueror of India when after a deep study of the Indian philosophy he wrote to the president of the East India Company saying: "...The writers of the Indian philosophies will survive, when the British dominion in India shall long have ceased to exist, and when the sources which it yielded of wealth and power are lost to remembrances." And a similar hope is shared by one of the greatest historians of the world, Arnold Toynbee, who said in an address delivered at Edinburgh University in 1952 that: "... In fifty years the world would be under the hegemony of the United States but in the twenty-first century, as religion captures the place of technology, it is possible that India the conquered will conquer its conquerors."

After centuries of spiritual meditations, the Indian sages and saints have concluded that "Shantih" (peace) is the only choice the mankind has for a happy living on this earth. But the peace is not possible if there is hunger in any part of the world, and people do not get justice or equality; and if might of the stronger country continues to be its right in the international community. Eradication of hunger, injustice and war has, therefore, become the paramount concern of not only the good people, but of all the people and countries of the world in their own interest because of the easy availability of the atom power in the hands of the rich and the strong or their allies the poor and the weak who can destroy the whole world in one minute. Hence the need for a religion of peace in stead of war; and the need for chanting the Hindu benediction of "Shantih, Shantih, Shantih."

A question should arise as to how the so called Hindu "religion" will work out the program or what will be the means to achieve the goal that it promises to the people of the world. There is no new method that the Hinduism will employ. It will show to the world the same ways and values that the classical reformers and teachers have been employing in times of need, and emphasizing the practice of them in the lives of the people of the world. It will not be a process to be handled by public lectures from the platform or the media; it will be a massive program to educate spiritually handicapped individuals into the basic commandments of Hindu dharma which will seize them and condition them so that they will refrain from wrong doings.

Obviously, it is not a one shot deal or a doze of medication to eradicate a bodily ailment, it is an ongoing process to repel the continuous mist of materialism or maya that clouds the minds of people. Materialism or maya captivates and corrupts humans so that they are confused, deluded and lost to themselves and to the society. Imagine if a plain looking glass is allowed to stay in a dust storm, it is natural that it will be completely buried in dust and lost. With more and more dust of materialism (maya) accumulated on the person of the individual, his soul will not only be polluted but he will be totally lost in the delusions of kam, krodh, lobh, and moha which are the perilous four doors of hell. It is the impact of materialism (maya) that causes conflicts which turn into wars threatening annihilation of the whole world. Materialism in individuals finds expression in private aims, passions, and satisfaction of selfish desires which have to be controlled or disciplined as a prerequisite for the conditioning of the individual mind and soul for the ultimate goal of moksha. Hindu thought attempts at employing unique behavior modification techniques or conditioning processes which takes us to the study of the yogas or experimental psychology.

Preface

Because no external force or discipline can curb the propensities of human nature permanently, continuous practice for perfection is the only means to diffuse or calm down the continuing impact of selfish aims and passions continuously demonstrated by each new arrival into this world. With more new arrivals than departures, the attitudinal and behavior problems keep multiplying resulting in the number of conflicts, violent showdowns and ultimate wars on national and international levels. Hindu thought is known to curb such tendencies by continuous process of repellants or preventives through meditation and yoga, including unselfish works and worship.

This book is intended primarily for the persons of India, who were never taught, in any formal way, through school education or religious teaching in their temples, the meaning of Hinduism, and for those non-Hindus around the world, who may be puzzled in their ignorance about the biggest religion of the world (Buddhism being one of the federating parts), and yet not bound by a dogma or an authoritarian doctrine so essential to their own religions. Surprisingly, when the absence of prophets would reduce a western religion to non-religion, and make their followers heretics, if they don't accept them as the only intermediaries between themselves and God, the disbelief in a prophet or incarnation or its substitution by a more favorable deity by a Hindu or doubting His very existence, as an anthropomorphic being, is neither sinful nor entails excommunication by this amazingly secular society.

Need for such a book was continuously felt by the author when, teaching in New York for several decades, he painfully observed non-Hindus completely ignorant of Hinduism, and Hindus, equally confused of their identity, and not only shirking to introduce themselves as Hindus, but also unable to give any definition of Hinduism, and came across several "Jacksons","Pauls", "Siegals", "Auroras", and "Karens" who suffering from their religious ignorance, tried to hide their Hindu names respectively as Jai Kishans, Pals, Sehgals, Aroras, and Kirans, in order to improve their images by identifying themselves with similar non-Hindu names.

Some of the young men have been heard saying not only in foreign countries but in India as well that they do not really know what Hinduism exactly is, and whom to worship among hundreds of deities from Krishna to cow. Well, they can say so, as the elders have yet to give them a simple education in Hinduism in their homes, or at least start telling them that in Hinduism all living beings are divine, in more or less degrees, and that it does not recommend worship of any particular god though none is forbidden. Further that the Hinduism expects its young men to find for themselves all about it when they have all the facilities in these modern times. Imagine, with no such help, Homer blindly "plagiarized" the Mahabharata; Pythagoras, Kant, Hegal, and Shopenhauer drew freely upon Kapila's Sankhya shashtra; and Thoreau, Emerson, and many others in far off America made Advaita as their way of life.

It is my belief that this book will not only give the reader a much needed information on the whole gamut of Hinduism based on the Vedas, traversing into the philosophies of the Upanishads summarized in the Bhagvadgita, but also transport them to heights beyond the reaches the Bhagvadgita, but also transport them to heights beyond the reaches of other literatures naturally sharing greatness with hundreds of seers like Buddha, Samkra and Gandhi. I shall have been truly rewarded in my effort if my readers would be inspired into a resolve to learn and help others know more about Hinduism.

A TYPICAL HINDU SCHOOL IN CLASSICAL PERIOD

ॐ पूर्णमदः पूर्णमिदं पूर्णात् पूर्णमुदच्यते । पूर्णस्य पूर्णमादाय पूर्णमेवावशिष्यते ॥

A FEW ARYAN CHARACTERS FROM THE EPIC RAMAYANA

THE HINDU ARYANS

Before trying to write about their thought, it is but proper to give an introduction about this wonderful society, known as Hindus, that gave the world a Krishna, a Buddha, a Gandhi, and hundreds of equally great saints, seers and scholars from Valmiki and Ved Vyasa to Samkra, Tulsidasa and Vivekananda, and with them a most logical, scientific and secular philosophy[1] of religion and free worship of God or free contemplation of the supernatural - something different from dogmas and creeds based on miracles, mysteries, and irrational stories. The Hindus are primarily Aryans, but got mixed up with Dravadians, ever since the Aryans moved around from their base in the North of India. Anatomically the people of India are closely related to the people of Europe. They look like them in the shape of their heads, in the shape of their noses, in the type of the hair they have.... They are called Caucasians.[2]

Most historians regard Hindus as that branch of the Aryan people who once lived together with other Aryan people under one roof in the Central Asian plains and migrated southward while all their kinsmen had earlier moved northward into the European plains and seashores. The evidence of language roots, grammar, words, myths, and legends unquestionably proves the popular theories that these Hindu Aryans had a common origin with the Celts, the Germans, the Slavokians, the Greeks, and the Persians. But some historians while

---

[1] Advaita is the greatest invention of Hindu mind in the domain of metaphysics.

[2] Waltr Bateman, How Man Began, p. 54

agreeing to a common base of all Aryan people, do not subscribe to the southward migration of the Hindu Aryans. Instead, they contend that the North of Indian peninsula was the original home of all Aryan people who, for `pastures new' moved westward from time to time leaving behind their more lethargic `elder brother' in `meditation' over the problems of life, death, life after death, and salvation. Since the trend of migration all over the world has been from East to West or from hotter regions to colder regions, or from densely populated areas to areas of sparse population, it is logical to deduce that North India was the Eastern home of migrating Caucasian people. Agreeing with this view Jules Michelet says: "Follow the migration of mankind from East to West along the sun's course and along the track of the world's magnetic currents; observe its long voyage from Asia to Europe, from India to France...At its starting point in India, the birthplace of races and religions, the womb of the world..." [1]

Although it has been the contention of several bio-geographical writers that the original homeland of the Aryan race was the Central Asia where they presumed was the human cradle, emotional leaning apart, it does not satisfy the "basic requirement" criteria for the early man to be a spot "where the warmth of the air was such that no clothing was necessary and where there were no wild beasts to endanger their safety. This argument found favor with several writers, especially the German biologist Haeckel who acknowledged that the human cradle was in the region of modern Afghanistan and Pakistan. Haeckel came out close to Kant's determination that this human cradle was around Shanghai and Delhi in North India. Since Kant and Haeckel are acceptable to the provisions of ancient Hindu scriptures, it is probable that Aryans had their common ancestral home in the North of India; and since it is the general consensus that the early man evolved

---

[1] Jules Michelet, <u>History of Rome,</u> p. 15

and lived in hotter regions, as the cold regions were unhabitable then, it is very possible that all Caucasians, including Aryans, had been moving to the colder North where, in the course of the millenniums, they turned ascendingly whiter.

Agreeing with the above historians, this author believes that the original home of the Sanskrit speaking Aryan race was India where Sanskrit has been the language of their scriptures, speech, and treasure house of creative literature from times immemorial. Although Sanskrit language is traceable all over the Caucasian lands in one mutilated form or another, it has stayed distinctly original, solid, and dense in a variety of forms from the primary to the most perfect form of the great grammarian Rishi Panini in India which then included the North and the West of the present day India. What this means is that the Aryans although lived not only in the areas south of Russia or in Central Asia but their original home was North India, including Nepal and Kashmir. From this base, they moved Northwest up to the northern regions of Europe, and the southeast of India up to Japan and Mongolia to establish for themselves an Indic society.

Sanskrit language is the main and unbroken link of kinship between these Aryan Hindus of India in the East and the western Caucasian races of Europe and the white Americans. Max Muller explains the relationship thus: "As the language of the Veda, the Sanskrit is the most ancient type of the English of the present day, (Sanskrit and English are but varieties of one and the same language), so its thoughts and feelings contain in reality the first roots and germs of that intellectual growth which by an unbroken chain connects our own generation with the ancestors of the Aryan race.[1] Will Durant gives it a wider basis: "We feel for a moment a strange sense of cultural continuity across great stretches of time and space when we observe the similarity - in Sanskrit, Greek and Latin and English - of the numeral, the family terms, and those insinuating little words that, by some oversight of the moralists, have been called the copulative verbs."[2]

Unquestionably, Sanskrit has a mother-daughter relationship with almost all European languages, including those of Iran, Turkey and southern Russia. And even though all these countries are now culturally different from each other, and almost all of them seem to have forgotten their Vedic heritage after being proselytized to other religions, there still remains the indelible imprint of Vedic Aryanism about them. According to H. G. Wells, "...All these languages have a common resemblance, as each, as we have already explained, rings the changes upon a number of common roots. When we find the same root word running through all or most of these languages, it seems reasonable to conclude that the thing the root word signifies must have been known to the common ancestors."[3] The following table illustrates the point:

Sanskrit	Persian	Latin	Greek	German	English
asmi	sum	aimi	bin	astam	am
asi	es	ei	bist	asti	are
asti	est	esti	i st	ast	is
pitar	pater	pater	vater	pitar	father
nama	nomen	onoma	nahme	nama	name

---

[1] Max Muller, The Vedas, p. 13

[2] Will Durant, Our Oriental Heritage, p. 406

[3] H.G. Wells, The outline of History, p.240

matri	mater	meter	mutter	matar		mother
bhratari	frater	phratar	bruder	bratar		brother

And so is the similarity in numerals as compared below:

English: one, two, three, four, five.

Sanskrit: ek, dwe, tree, chatur, pancham.

Greek: heis, due, tria, tettara, pente.

Latin: unus, duo, tres, quattuor, quinque.

We can go on and on, but this comparison should be sufficient to establish that the Aryan people had one common tongue and one ancestral origin at one point of time.

This ancestral home of the Aryans, as per Hindu scriptures, was the area between Kabul in Afghanistan and the upper Ganges where they had built up small kingdoms mostly under hereditary monarchs. "The center of this Aryan world was the firm middle country (dhruva madhyama dis) stretching from the Saraswati (now only seasonal, flows near Kurukshetra) to the Gangetic Doab and occupied by the Kurus, the Panchalas and some adjoining tribes. It was from this region that Brahmanical civilization spread to the outer provinces, to the land of the Kosalas and the Kasis drained by the Sarayu and the Varanavati, to the swamps east of the Gandak colonized by the Videhas, and to the valley of the Wardha occupied by the Vidarbhas. Beyond them lived the tribes of mixed origin like the Angas of East Behar and the Magadhas of South Bihar, as well as Dasyus or aboriginal folk like the Pundras of North Bengal, the Pulindas and Savaras of the Vindhyan forest, and the Andhras in the Valley of the Godavari."[1]

Most people living in the South Indian peninsula are ethnically different from most Aryan stock in the North. They speak languages - Tamil, Telugu, Kanarese and Malyalam – and are generally known as "Dravadians". The Dravida or Tamil country had its independent polity side by side with the Aryans of North India, and had important kings from Chola and Pandya dynasties known as far back as the second century B.C. if not earlier. Despite racial differences, Brahmanism (Hinduism) spread in the South as the Aryans moved southward absorbing the people into their religious and cultural fold and being absorbed into theirs. They learned southern languages for better communication and to interpret scriptures to the masses in the South.

Political or racial conflicts with the southern potentates were not infrequent. The legendary non-Aryan king Ravana's incursions in the Aryan North compelling Rama to punish him by invading Lanka could be racially inspired or politically motivated. The story of Rama popularly known as The Ramayana was one of many heroic stories of the Aryan kings who fought battles with the southern rulers in the process of the colonization of the South in those very early days of the Aryan expansion. Incidentally, this epic story which by virtue of its theme and literary rendering by its author Rishi Valmiki and later by Saint Tulsidas and other well-known poets who retold it in their regional vernacular poetry rose in popularity to the heights equal to the Bible in the Christian world, and became the standard of Hindu idealism and Sanatan Dharma with the finest precepts from the Hindu scriptures. The story is supposed to be earlier in time than the other great epic, the Mahabharata. Both these stories are retold briefly at the end of this book.

---

[1] R. C. Majumdar, An Advanced History of India, p. 40

Even after the South was dominated religiously and culturally by the Aryan North, integration of the fast increasing multiracial population was a continuing dilemma of the thinking elite of the Aryan race who wanted to preserve their white color (varna dharma) despite the religious and cultural unity of the people. Their answer to this problem was perhaps the well-known `caste system' which they formally enforced by law and religion. The society was likened to the human body that functions through the thinking head, muscle power, body-power building stomach and the servicing legs. The caste system of India was originally designed along the same lines and was enforced to regulate efficient working of the society; but it seems that in course of time the process was given a rational 'quality work' (gun - karm) basis for the four sections of the society: Brahman, Kshatriya, Vaish and Shudra. Some earliest sources have attributed it to the gun - dharm of the people based on their merit in meditation (Ardhana shakti) which makes up the rope of material nature. Thus a person with preponderance of dullnesss or sloth (tams) was known as shudra, the one with attributes of passion or energy (rajas) was called Vaishya or Kshatriya, and the one on the highest step of the ladder with most attributes of goodness or purity (sattava) was known as brahman. Shrimad Bhagvadgita recognizes this view in Chapter 4.13. Whatever the basis, the society got classified into four divisions:

(1) Brahmans who were philosophers and priests,
(2) Kshatriyas who were warriors and fighting people,
(3) Vaishyas who were agriculturists and merchants, and
(4) Shudras who were janitors and service class.

The first three groups were made up of Aryan blood, but the fourth was not supposed to be Aryan. With emphasis on the work performed, this system did regulate the society and kept the Aryan blood pure for a long time. That is why this extraordinary scheme, given its divine semblance, has been classed among the greatest expressions of human ingenuity.

But the caste system deteriorated like any other human institution in course of time as it stopped the inter-caste mobility of the higher classes who were reluctant to do the work of a lower caste. Hence the status of a person became known by his birth rather than by his work. Higher castes became conscious of their superior social status of which they felt proud. Foreign invasions made the castes more rigid and Hinduism more worthy of protection from these invaders who always destroyed other religions and their believers. Thus, more and more Hindu Aryans shifted to the South to protect their culture where they found new philosophers and interpreters of their scriptures. But to avoid racial hostility, they prudently played low on their Aryan heritage, and let the entire population be known by whatever name became popular in course of time. As by now the Aryans in the North had been known as Hindus (corrupted from Sindhus, Indus, the name given by the invading Greeks to the people living across the river Sindhu), the name Hindu found easy acceptance by all the population of the sub-continent most of which had been mixed up in the fast-moving melting pot.

These Hindu Aryans generally lived a settled, peaceful life for a number of centuries since the prolific soil gave them all they wanted: "The history of India for many centuries had been happier, less fierce, and more dreamlike than any other history."[1] In these favorable conditions, they built a character - meditative and peaceful and a "nation of philosophers such as could nowhere have existed except in

---

[1] H. G. Wells, The Outlines of History, p. 855

India."[2] This is not to say that India did not have big disturbances. Indian peaceful life was occasionally disrupted before or after the "peaceful" period as apart from regional disturbances, India was invaded from across her western borders, time and again, by Greeks, Shaks, Huns, Arabs, Pathans, Mongols, etc. and some of her areas remained under foreign rule for centuries together. But even under grievous persecutions from the ruling foreigners, especially Moslems, the basics of its civilization remained undefiled and, as soon as the crises were over, its people returned to the same old ways of searching for the perfection or the unknown - a passion so aptly described by Irwin Babbit in the following verse:

> *"East bowed low before the blast*
> *In humble deep disdain,*
> *It let the legions thunder past*
> *And plunged in thought again."*

India, at the zenith of its glory under Guptas, began degenerating fast after the death of king Harsha in 646 A.D., and had its religion, culture, and peaceful life completely disturbed by invaders, especially Moslems from across its western borders beginning 10th century A.D. The entire northwestern India (the present Pakistan which still was a strong Hindu people); and later, of course, the rest of India was gradually butchered and plundered with ruthless savagery surpassing perhaps even the genocide in the Americas. This was done to the people who always respected other religions and cultures and, if ever went out of their country, they went as teachers and religious preachers in safron robes just to teach peace and non-violence. But

---

[2] Max Muller, The Vedas, p.3

these were the dark ages when the whole world was going through the trauma caused by new adventurers and fanatic kings who though primarily motivated by Indian wealth or personal ambitions started to conquer Indian lands, but ended up in their resolve to destroy the Indian people and their culture as well. Elsewhere in Europe these adventures got transformed into long drawn full-scale religious wars ignoring the lofty and noble precepts of their great prophets. Almost all historians are unanimous on the facts, but more forthright of them all, Arthur Schopenhauer narrates the sordid tale as follows:

"...This of the fanaticism, the endless persecutions, the religious wars, that sanguinary frenzy of which the ancients had no conception! think of the crusades, a butchery lasting two hundred years and inexcusable, its war cry `It is the will of God,' its object to gain possession of the grave of one who preached love and sufferance! think of the cruel expulsion and extermination of the Moors and Jews from Spain! Think of the orgies of blood, the inquisitions, the heretical tribunals, the bloody and terrible conquests ...in three continents, or... in America, whose inhabitants were for the most part, and in Cuba entirely, exterminated. According to Las Cases, Christianity murdered twelve millions in forty years, of course all in majorem Dei gloriam, and for the propagation of the Gospel, and because what wasn't Christian wasn't even looked upon as human! I have, it is true, touched upon these matters before; but in our day, we hear of Latest News from the Kingdom of God, we shall not be weary of bringing old news to mind. And above all, don't let us forget India, the cradle of the human race, or at least of that part of it to which we belong, where first ... were most cruelly infuriated against the adherents of the original faith of mankind. The destruction or disfigurement of the ancient temples and idols, a lamentable, mischievous and barbarous act still bears witness to the monotheistic fury ... carried on from Mahmud, the Ghaznevid of cursed memory, down to Aureng Zeb, the fratricide, whom the Portuguese Christians have zealously imitated by destruction of temples and the auto de fe of the inquisition at Goa...."For the sake of truth, I must add that the fanatical enormities perpetrated in the name of religion are only to be put down to the adherents of monotheistic creeds.... We hear nothing of the kind in the case of Hindoos and Buddhists. Although it is a matter of common knowledge that about the fifth century of our era Buddhism was driven out by the Brahmans from its ancient home in the southernmost part of the Indian peninsula, and afterwards spread over the whole of the rest of Asia, as far as I know, we have no definite account of any crimes of violence, or wars or cruelties, perpetrated in the course of it."[1]

BUDDHA
HIS LOFTY TEACHINGS OF COMPASSION AND NON-VIOLENCE UNNERVED THE NATION TO FACILITATE FOREIGN INVASIONS!

---

[1] T. Bailey Saunders, The Essays of Arthur Schopenhauer, p. 42 - 43

BORROWINGS BY WESTERNERS
IN PHILOSOPHY, ARTS, MATHEMATICS AND SCIENCES

"… But hardly the British established themselves in India before editions and translations of the Upanishads began to stir Western thought. Fichte conceived an idealism strangely like Shankra's; Schopenhauer almost incorporated Buddhism, the Upanishads and the Vedanta into his philosophy; and Schelling, in his old age, thought the Upanishads the maturest wisdom of mankind."

                    Will Durant

"While the opinion that Greek thought has been influenced by the Indian is frequently held, it is not so often urged that Indian thought owes much to Greek speculation."

                    Professor Garbe

HINDU CONTRIBUTIONS

"... The Indians never went to ask anything from other nations."[1] In fact, they September 11, 1893, Swami Vivekanand declared thus: "... I am proud to belong to a nation which has sheltered the persecuted and the refugees of all religions and all nations of the earth. I am proud to tell you that we have gathered in our bosom the purest remnant of the Israelites, who came to Southern India and took refuge with us in the very year in which their holy temple was shattered to pieces by Roman tyranny. I am proud to belong to the religion which has sheltered and is still fostering the remnant of the great Zoroastrian nation."[2] In return for all this, they suffered wholesale robberies and butcheries at the hands of almost all foreigners. Yet they kept themselves absorbed in building a peaceful society and civilization, primarily spiritual and humane, and developing arts and sciences which were the envy of the whole world. And in the confines of their homes, these thinking people produced the finest first in the domain of literature, philosophy, music, architecture, mathematics, medicine, astronomy, physics, chemistry and surgery which, as per most unbiased scholars, became the source and inspiration of most of the western world.

In classical times, beside mutual trade relations, Indian scholars had spread in almost all countries around India; and western students flocked to Indian universities for education. "Students flocked to Taxila as in the Middle Ages they flocked to Paris; there all the arts and sciences could be studied under eminent professors, and the medical

---

[1] Voltaire, Philosophy of History, p.74

[2] Complete Works of Swami Vivekananda, p.3

school especially was held in high repute throughout the Oriental world."¹

Indians had good "contacts with Greece and neighboring countries long before Alexander came to the East as Panini who wrote his great grammar of Sanskrit language as early as the sixth or seventh century B.C. had mentioned the Greek script."² ". . . Buddhism at the time was a proselytizing religion. Asoka (269-232 B.C.), the saintly Buddhist king, records in a still extant inscription, that he sent missionaries to all the Macedonian kings: `And this is the chiefest conquest in His Majesty's opinion the conquest by the Law.'"³ These contacts gave rise to certain borrowings by both sides. Learned Indians used to go to Greece to discuss questions of philosophy with Socrates and other philosophers. According to Will Durant Plato was known to have roamed the Indian centers of learning and studied Yoga at Benaras. Jawaharlal Nehru wrote in his Discovery of India that "Pythagoras was particularly influenced by Indian philosophy and Professor H.G. Rawlinson remarks that 'almost all the theories, religious, philosophical, and mathematical, taught by the Pythagorians were known in India in the sixth century B.C.' A European classical scholar, Urwick, has based his interpretation of the 'Republic' of Plato upon Indian thought."⁴

According to Will Durant, "Among the most vital parts of our Oriental heritage are the `Arabic' numerals and the decimal system, both of

---

[1] Will Durant, Our Oriental Heritage
[2] Jawaharlal Nehru, Discovery of India, p.69
[3] Bertrand Russell, A History of Western Philosophy , p.222
[4] Jawaharlal, Nehru, Discovery of India, p. 155

which came to us, through the Arabs, from India. The miscalled `Arabic' numerals are found on the Rock Edicts of Asoka (256 B.C.), a thousand years before their occurrence in Arabic literature, said the great and magnanimous Laplace:

`It is India that gave us the ingenious method of expressing all numbers by ten symbols, each receiving a value of position as well as an absolute value; a profound and important idea which appears so simple to us now that we ignore its true merit. But its very simplicity, the great ease which it has lent to all computations, puts our arithmetic in the first rank of useful inventions; and we shall appreciate the grandeur of its achievement the more when we remember that it escaped the genius of Archimedes and Apollonius, two of the greatest men produced by antiquity.'

The decimal system was known to Aryabhata and Brahmagupta long before its appearance in the writings of the Arabs and the Syrians; it was adopted by China from Buddhist missionaries."[1] According to Voltaire, "The Greeks, before the time of Pythagoras, traveled into India for instruction. The signs of the seven planets and of the seven metals are still almost all over the earth, such as the Indians invented: the Arabians were obliged to adopt their cyphers."[2] They called the Indian numbers as "Hindse" meaning "from India". Over one thousand years before Voltaire, Severus Sebokht, a Syrian astronomer - monk wrote the following in A.D. 662, as quoted by A.L. Bhasham in his

---

[1] Will Durant, Our Oriental Heritage, p. 527

[2] Voltaire, Philosophy of History, p.527

wellknown book on India.[1]

"I shall now speak of the knowledge of the Hindus...of their subtle discoveries in the science of astronomy - discoveries even more ingenious than those of the Greeks and Babylonians - of their rational system of mathematics or of their method of calculation which no word can praise strongly enough - I mean the system using nine symbols. If these things were known by the people who think that they alone have mastered the sciences because they speak Greek, they would perhaps be convinced that every folk, not only Greeks, but men of a different tongue, know something as well as they."

An important Mathematics book prescribed by the New York State Education Department acknowledges the debt in the following words:

"The Western world owes a great deal to India for a simple invention. It was developed by an unknown Indian more than 1500 years ago. Without it most of the great discoveries and inventions of western civilization would never have come about. This invention was the decimal system of numerals - nine digits and a zero. The science and technology of today could not have developed if we had only had the Roman system of numerals. That system is too clumsy to be used as a scientific tool. [2] For a long time the Hindu numerals were called as "Arabic numerals" because they had reached West through the invading Arabs; but it is not so : these numerals that are the basis of our sciences, mathematics and economy, were really invented by the

---

[1] A. L. Bhasham, The Wonder That Was India, p.vi
[2] Harry Shor and Gloria Meng, Exploring Algebra, p.ix

mathematicians of India as the grateful Arabs have named them "Hindse" which means "from India." It is generally believed that the decimal system appears in Indian records from 4th century A.D., but the Indian scholars believe that Hindus used their numbers from times immemorial!

Jacolliot feels India has given to the West much more than she is credited with when he says: "Besides the discoverers of geometry and algebra, the constructors of human speech, the parents of philosophy, the primal expounders of religion, the adepts in psychological and physical science, how even the greatest of our biologists and theologians seem dwarfed! Name to us any modern discovery, and we venture to say that Indian history need not long be searched before the prototype will be found on record. Here we are with the transit of science half accomplished, and all our vedic ideas in process of readjustment to the theories of force correlation, natural selection, atomic polarity and evolution. And here, to mock our conceit, our apprehensions, and our despair, we may read what Manu said, perhaps 10,000 years before the birth of Christ:

"The first germ of life was developed by water and heat. (Book I, slokas 8, 9). Water ascends toward the sky in vapors; from the sun it descends in rain, from the rains are born the plants, and from the plants, animals. (Book III, sloka 76)."[1]

Borrowings by western scholars in the sphere of literature and philosophy are obvious and well-known. There are near virtual copies [2]

---

[1] Louis Jacolliot, Krishna and Christ, p.15
[2] Bernard V. Van Nooten, The Mahabharata, p.109

of plots, characters, episodes, situations and time duration from the Mahabharata in Homer and Virgil. Similarly, the laws of Manu and the six complete systems of Hindu Philosophy and Political Science premonish all that Pythagoras, Aristotle, Lamark, Kant, Hegel, Shopenhauer, Freud and Marx have written thousands of years later. And Hindu mythology is replete with descriptions showing that Hindu seers have spiritually seen the Whole Truth which the scientists are clamoring to experiment physically.

Victor Cousin believes that "we are constrained to see in this cradle of human race the native land of the highest philosophy."[1] Max Muller was all praise for Schopenhauer's truthfulness as Schopenhauer was all praise for the truth of the Upanishads when he writes: "In the whole world there is no study so beneficial and so elevating as that of the Upanishads. It has been the solace of my life -it will be the solace of my death."[2] Warren Hastings, the conqueror of India next after Clive and her Governor General, was so much impressed with Hindu philosophy that he engaged a Sanskrit teacher to teach himself Sanskrit and Vedanta. He later wrote a preface to the Charles Wilkins' translation of the Bhagvadgita and recommended it to the President of the East India Company declaring that ". . .The writers of the Indian philosophies will survive, when the British dominion in India shall long have ceased to exist, and when the sources which it yielded of wealth and power are lost to remembrances."[3]

Max Muller wants the white race for a truly human and eternal life to make amends and stop living their lives with Greek, Roman and

---

[1] Will Durant, Our Oriental Heritage, p. 109
[2] Max Muller, The Vedas, p. 151
[3] Romain Rolland, Life and Gospel of Swami Vivekananda, p.49

Jewish thought, but instead, to adopt the Hindu way of life: ". . .If I were asked under what sky the human mind has most fully developed some of its choicest gifts, has most deeply pondered over the greatest problems of life, and has found solutions of some of them which well deserve the attention even of those who have studied Plato and Kant, I should point to India. And if I were to ask myself from what literature, we here in Europe, we who have been nurtured almost exclusively on the thoughts of Greeks and Romans, and one Semitic race, the Jewish, may draw the corrective which is most wanted in order to make our inner life more truly human a life, not for this life only, but a transfigured and eternal life - again I should point to India. [1] Keyserling has "not found in Europe or America, poets, thinkers or popular leaders equal, or even comparable, to those of India today."[2] Romain Rolland wants his European brethren to return to their original home for peace and fulfillment in their mother's nest: "Let us return to our eagle's nest in the Himalayas. It is waiting for us, for it is ours, eaglets of Europe, we need not renounce any part of our real nature. . .whence we formerly took our flight."[3] Will Durant would like the West to learn from India tolerance and gentleness and love for all living things: "Perhaps in return for conquest, arrogance and spoilation, India will teach us the tolerance and gentleness of the mature mind, the quiet content of the unacquisitive soul, the calm of the understanding spirit, and a unifying, a

---

[1] Quoted from Jawaharlal Nehru's Discovery of India, p. 54

[2] Count H. Keyserling, Travel diary of a Philosopher, p.265

3. Romain Rolland, Life and Gospel of Vivekananda, p.295

pacifying love for all living things."[1]

Just as treasures of gold and jewels must be protected by strong security measures, this precious heritage of mankind had to have an all-time strong political deterrent for the rapacious barbarians. It couldn't be done. So this Hindu nation developed complacency, neglected the more important rules of political philosophy - strength of arms and defensive preparedness, weakened themselves in internal divisions, forgot the doctrine of Karma Yoga so central to their thought, took refuge in supernatural consolations and practiced religions like Jainism and Budhism which removed them away from the realities of life. They, therefore, failed to organize unitedly to defend their frontiers when the invasions came. The result was that legion after legion of western barbarians invaded India with avarice and holy zeal for nearly one thousand years. While the non-Europeans, in holy frenzy, slaughtered millions of Hindus and proselytized a large number of them in the then India from Baluchistan to Bengal and pillaged and burnt their cities, and centuries old civilization by destroyed their temples and religious books, and carried their accumulated treasures of wealth and women population for sale, the Europeans behaved a bit better inasmuch as they neither destroyed temples nor raped women nor slaughtered people in large numbers. Their subtle and crafty ways just conquered the whole of India by sucking out more wealth than all their predecessors had done together by brute force.

Lamenting this bloodiest story in history, Will Durant advises peace loving people never to trust the barbarians again and be always prepared to pay the price of civilization: "The bitter lesson that may be

---

[1] . Will Durant, <u>Our Oriental Heritage,</u> p. 633

drawn from this tragedy is that eternal vigilance is the price of civilization. A nation must love peace, but keep its powder dry.[1]

SHIVAJI BHONSLE
WHO ROSE TO DESTROY THE CRUEL MIGHTY MOGHUL EMPIRE IN ORDER TO LIBERATE THE MUCH PERSECUTED HINDU NATION.

---

[1] Will Durant, Our Oriental Heritage, p.463

AUM

THE FOUR VEDAS:

RIG VEDA
YAJUR VEDA
SAM VEDA
ATHARVA VEDA

HINDUISM – ITS SOURCES

Hinduism may not be called religion in the sense other religions are known. "It is much more than a religion; it is a total way of life, incorporating the customs, beliefs, practices, institutions of the people in all parts of the sub-continent developed at all periods of human settlement there. As a religion, Hinduism has set side by side in peaceful coexistence every shade of belief ranging from the most primitive sort of animism to a highly sophisticated philosophical monism, and with this has gone a corresponding range of worship of practice extending from the simplest disease spirits to the most concentrated meditation designed to produce knowledge of abstract impersonal reality.[1] Swami Vivekanand describes it thus: "From the high spiritual flights of the Vedanta philosophy, of which the latest discoveries of science seem like echoes, to the low ideas of idolatry with its multifarious mythology, the agnosticism of the Buddhists, and the atheism of the Jains, each and all have a place in the Hindu's religion.[2]

Unlike other religions, Hinduism has no founder. It does not depend for its authority on the personality of any man - a messiah, a savior, a prophet, or a guru. Its authority is eternal Truth which has revealed itself through the minds of great rishis who perfected themselves by long penances and are said to have heard in their hearts eternal truths as Sruti. Thus it has become a cumulative record of metaphysical experimentation.

It is believed by the orthodox theologians that not a single Veda is the work of the human mind as they were revealed by the deity. This

---

[1] W. Norman Brown, Mythology of India, p.280
[2] Complete Works of Swami Viveknanda, Vol. 1, p.6

claim is valid because in Hinduism a deity is a perfected master or a supernatural being capable of saying eternal truths. The various mythological gods were once humans who were elevated to gods and goddesses through service, and later incarnated themselves as humans; and no wonder they were the persons who revealed the truths which are expressed in the Vedas. We all are very familiar with Shrimad Bhagvadgita which is composed of lectures given by His incarnate Lord Krishna to Arjuna. The earlier truths expressed in the Vedas were essentially the same though spoken in different context. In fact, to Hindus, all truths have been Vedas and those who said them were divine beings. Is not Ramakrishana Paramhamsa regarded as a divine being even by the great intellectuals of modern times? And wasn't Gandhi about to be deified by the masses but for a very strong resistance from those who knew Gandhi's views against such a move? Truths spoken now can become Sruti a few thousand years later.

Vedas are also called Sruti meaning voices that were heard by spiritual masters. They are classified and named as: the Rgveda, the Samaveda, the Yajurveda and the Atharvaveda. Each Veda consists of three parts: (i) the Mantra or hymns, (ii) the Brahmanas or explanatory treatises on mantras and rituals and (iii) the Upanishada or mystic treatises revealing the most profound spiritual truths and suggesting the ways of realizing them. Just as the flower of fruit is the most important part of the plant, so are the Upanishadas the most important part of the vedas. They are many, but the most important of them all are twelve: namely - Isa, Kena, Katha, Prasna, Mundaka, Mandukya, Aitareya, Taittiriya, Chandogya, Brhadranyaka, Kausitki, and Svetasvatara.

Rgveda is the Veda par excellence, the real veda that traces the earliest growth of religious ideas in India. It is the earliest book of the Hindus and, indeed, of the whole world. It is in poetical form, has one thousand twenty eight poems or hymns called Samhita. It is so much full of thought that at this early period in history no poet in any other nation could have conceived them. The sublimity, the nobility, the natural justice, the equality, the love and welfare of all humanity as a whole is the theme of the Rgveda. The Vedic God has no partisan attitude of the jealous and vindictive God, who is ever ready to please and help his own people by hurling disease, death and destruction on their enemies in return for sacrifices. There is no idolatry in the Vedas; and no temples for the gods. It appears the Indian society in those days had already traversed from polytheism and monotheism to abstract monism. "Rgvada is the earliest book that humanity possesses. Yet behind the Rgveda itself lay ages of civilized existence and thought during which had grown all other civilizations . . . . ."[1] Indian poetic thought at this stage appears as free, candid and honest about the nature of God as that of any modern thinker who would express the doubts and sorrows of his heart without any inhibition. There is also a refusal to be bound into any dogma about the supernatural though their ecstatic expressions do acknowledge Him as the Highest Being, as can be seen from this hymn of the Rgveda:

Hymn X, 129

Nor aught nor naught existed; you bright sky
all t there nothing since has been.
Darkness there was, and at first was veiled
In gloom profound, an ocean without light;
The germ that still lay covered in the husk,
Burst forth, one nature, from the fervent heat.

---

[1] Jawaharlal Nehru, Discovery of India, p. 43

Then first came Love upon it, the new germ,
Of mind; yea, poets in their hearts discerned
And uncreated. Came this ray from earth
Piercing and all-pervading, or from heaven?
Then seeds were sown, and mighty powers arose,
Nature below, and Power and will above;
Who knows the secret? who proclaimed it here,
Whence, whence this manifold creation sprang?
The gods themselves came later into being,
Who knows from whence this great creation sprang?
He from whom all this great creation came,
Whether his will created or was mute,
The most high Seer that is in highest heaven,
He knows it - or perchance even He knows not.[1]

Literature mirrors its society. We can see through the books of a people its gods, its beliefs, its manners, its customs and its indulgences leading to the goals of its people. Looking at modern times, even after European prosperity through colonization, slave trade and multinationals, the concept of universal love and welfare, as a guiding principle of man, is still elusive despite international temper of the oncoming twenty-first century. Looking at the savagery in African and Yogoslavian countries, it looks the people have not risen above the crusades in dark ages. In comparison, the vedic society, it appears, had long forgotten its racial and national bias, if any, so that it is clear from its literature that it was obsessed with no other concern and consideration but the welfare of all the living beings not just the welfare of some or of one's own countrymen, white, yellow or black. The

---

[1] Rg Veda, Creation Hymn X, 129, translated by Max Muller, The Veda, p.81

popular Vedic verse: "sarve bhawantu sukhinah sarve niramaya, sarve bhadrani pashyantu, ma kashchit dukkhamapnuyat" meaning: "let all be happy, let all be without greed or illusion; let all see the right and let no one be in pain, O Lord", has been the guiding principle of Hinduism. And to attain that goal the individual had to be motivated to shed ignorance and to work for divine life. Hence, another well-known Vedic invocation: "Lead me from the unreal to the real! Lead me from darkness to light! Lead me from death to immortality."

After Sruti - the Vedas, there are a number of secondary authorities based on the vedas. The first of these is Smrti mening those which were memorized. Smrti consists of human compositions trying to regulate individual and social life in accordance with the principles of the Sruti. Most important lawgivers of the Hindu society or the writers of Smrti are Manu, Yajnavalkya and Parasara. Their codes or compositions deal with the Dharma or the duty of the various classes of citizens. That is why their law books are called dharma-sastras. In these law books are mentioned the duties of a man according to his class and station in life and duties of the king, the administration of civil and criminal law and the punishment or penances for the defaulting persons. The laws of the Smrti too are subordinate to the external principles of the Sruti.

Next to the Smrtis or the codes of law are Itihasas, the Puranas, the Agamas and the Darsanas. Our Itihasas are the two well-known epics - the Ramayana and the Mahabharata. Their object is to bring home to the common man by means of history the principles of the Veda and the laws of the Smrti. The greatest characters portrayed in these epics have become for all times the source of inspiration and emulation for the members of the Hindu society and, indeed, for all societies since their approach is human with no consideration of race or place. The authors of these epics - Rishi Valmiki and Rishi Ved Vyasa were great sages and professors of our thought in two different ages, who, through their creations, created ideal and practical human beings struggling to solve problems of their times, and for all times indeed, since those problems are universal. The Mahabharta contains the famous lecture known as Shrimad Bhagvadgita which, in fact, is the essence of the Hindu thought spoken through the mouth of Lord Krishna Himself.

Important Puranas are eighteen in number of which the most popular are the Vishnu Purana and the Bhagavata Purana; the latter is considered as great as the Ramanaya and the Mahabharata. The Agamas are many in number and can be divided into three main groups according as the deity that forms the object of worship is Vishnu, Siva or Sakti. Three main branches of Hinduism, namely, Vaisnavism, Saivism and Saktism are important names of these groups. Vaisnavism glorified the Supreme Being under one of the names and forms of Vishnu; in Saivism Siva is the alternative of Godly powers, and the Saktism considers mother power the Supreme Being as the object of worship of its followers.

Darshanas are schools of Hindu philosophy which try to systematize the teachings of the various parts of the Vedas. In them the appeal is to the imagination, and in the Agamas the appeal is to the heart. The Darshanas are six: Nyaya, founded by Gautama; Vaisesika, founded by Kanada; Sankhya, founded by Kapila; Yoga, founded by Pantanjali; Mimamsa, founded by Jaimini; and Vedanta was founded by Badarayana. Vedanta system is based on the monistic philosophy of the universe and is the most representative metaphysical thought of the Hindus, which has been popularized by the great guru Shankracharya.

Buddhism, Jainism and other schools of materialistic thought, being originally reactions to the supremacy of the Vedas and Brahmanism, respectively doubting and denying the existence of God, preached non-violence and morality despising ritualism in the beginning but getting themselves caught into their own cobwebs. They flourished in India as reforming offshoots of Hinduism, but got absorbed in the latter leaving behind their philosophies but not many followers. Later sources of Hinduism are the commentaries of eminent philosophers and theologians like Samkara, Ramanuja and Madhava, which have given rise to various schools of Vedanta. Then saints and poets of vernacular languages from the medieval to the modern times have made invaluable contributions to the understanding of Hinduism for the masses since over the centuries Sanskrit, the language of the scriptures, was replaced by the regional vernaculars.

Saints like Ramakrishna Paramhansa, Dayananda, Vivekananda,Tagore, Aurobindo and Gandhi, etc. have shown the universal and non-sectarian character of Hinduism through their practices and preachings. The western scholars such as Charles Wilkins, William Jones, Max Muller, Colebrook, Schopenhauer, Romain Rolland, etc. in Europe and Emerson, Thoreau, Norman Brown, Troy Organ, and many more in the USA have greatly contributed to introducing Hinduism not only to the Westerners but also to the Indian intelligentsia who got to know much about Hinduism through the medium of English.

It does not end here, as Hinduism is not a closed book. It is a movement, as Dr. Radhakrishnan likes to call it. It is an ongoing experimentation in metaphysics through experimental psychology. It is a continuous struggle of the human mind to attain to the Super mind. While it does that, it continues to embrace and absorb other thoughts and dogmas lacking reason or scientific approach, hoping that at some day, this Advaita (Hinduism) of India super-adding itself to science, will bring lasting peace to the world by closing down all religious shops.

THE GURU AS GUIDE

भगवान् व्यासका पुराण-प्रवचन

THE GUIDES IN HINDU LITERATURE

Through the Vedic literature, the rishis, the spiritual masters concerned with reforming and regulating human conduct expressed their knowledge of the powers of good and evil in the universe which protect or punish living beings in accordance with the Law of Nature. Gods and demons became symbolic of these powers. The most important of the good ones are the gods popularly known as Brahma, Vishnu, Mahesh, and smaller ones from Devraj Indra downward to gandharvas, nags, kinnars, asuras, etc. - all of them great and powerful in their own right by their deeds and penances through which they attained their powers subject only to the paramount Law of Nature of the all powerful God Almighty, Brahman. Symbolizing evil are many demons or rakshasas. His Law of Nature is nothing but the just law of Karma, the Eternal Moral Order which is supposed to guide not only the Hindus but all beings, and guided by which He Himself is busy in His cyclic Cosmic Action. He affirms this in the Gita (Ch.3.22) saying:

> na me Parth' asti kartavyam trisu lokesu kimcana,
> na navaptam avaptavyam varta eva ca karmani

Meaning: "In the three worlds, O Partha, there is nothing that I need to do; or there is anything that I cannot attain, yet I continue working."

The Nature's forces appearing good or evil gods to our subjective minds are at war with each other. The evil ones are opposite of the good ones who are destined in the end to be victorious. Unless they are intellectuals with abstract philosophical interests, the common man or woman usually has a favorite god or goddess who are supposed to guide and support them. The Hindus emulate their gods and goddesses, and try to gain spiritual merit in more or less degrees on the belief that all living beings are graded higher or lower based on their karmas. Troy Organ believes that "the gradation aspect of the deva concept gives to Hinduism a pattern for integrating all living forms. The separation of animals, men and gods so essential to western religions, is rejected. In the Hebrew myth of Creation, the Creator asks the first man to name the animal as they are brought before him, i.e., to gain control over them, since the name is the power. This seems to the Hindu to separate and to oppose diametrically, beings who by nature and by right belong in the same line of evolutionary development. Perhaps the deva concept fits the theory of organic evolution better than the typical view of Western religions." This is the First Beyond of Nature, the First Guide.

The Second Beyond is the world of the departed spirits such as pitris, fathers, mothers, etc. whose presence continued to be felt by the children after the former were dead and gone. As all the living beings are extensions of their ancestors, they continue to cherish their ancestral memory and have spiritual relationship with them even after their death. This relationship is a necessary guide as Manu says: "On the path on which his fathers and grandfathers have walked, on that path of good men, let him walk, and he will not go wrong."[1] Among the pitris are the divines, sages and saints of our race, such as, Rama, Krishna, Manu, Vishwamitra, Vishishta, Yajnyavalkya, Parashra, Bhardwaja, Vyasa, Galava, Gautama, Patanjali, Kapila, Kanada, Buddha, Shamkra, Vivekananda, Aurobindo, Gandhi, and many more yet to arrive. Included also in them are characters, which the philosopher poets have created as ideal persons to act as our guides. For instance, in the Ramayana and the Mahabharata, a role model can be found for any father, mother, son, daughter, brother, husband, wife, friend, servant, king, queen, etc. as a good guide and a bad guide - the good guide always showing the way toward the one and the only one straight line. The institution of shradhas is a part of this Beyond. Hindus

---

[1] Manu Smiriti, IV, 178

commemorate their departed pitris and express feelings of their absence every year during the two weeks of `shradhas' when they feed the brahmans and the poor in the belief that the departed pitris will receive the offerings or the love thus transmitted wherever they will be as spirits or in body form.

As a corollary to Pitris is the institution of the Guru which has been guiding the Hindu in the variety of ways: a deity in the form of a statue or picture, a book, a living object , the spiritual master who is a symbol of perfection. The essence of this concept is based on the urge of the Hindu to emulate and be worthy of his perfect master, in flesh and blood, whom he can see face to face. The Hindu does not generally believe in miracles or stories of the spiritual masters. To him seeing is believing. In this context, the status of a perfect spiritual master is considered higher than a written book, the Veda, for instance: A real guru or a perfected being surpasses an earlier book or a written theory since as long as the minute spiritual monad has not become one with the Supreme Spirit, there is more to be added to the earlier statements. In the context of continuous improvement of the individual self, the following shloka (Ch.2.46) of The Bhagvad-gita is important:

> Yavan artha udapane sarvatah samplut'odake
> Tavan sarvesu vedesu brahmanasya vijanatah.

Meaning: The Vedas are not more useful to an enlightened Brahman than a water tank in a place covered all over with water. Even though this verse seems to reject the authority of the Vedas, it is not so in the context of the common people engaged in the spiritual exercise, because Vedas are the only guide for the humans; but it is so between the one earthly being and the enlightened one, and who has become 'Brahm' because he certainly has no need for the Vedas. The Vedas continue to be supreme for works leading to the heights of the paradise, but not for the 'mukta'.

There was another idea (guide) which was central to the ancient Hindu thought and adopted by the Hindu society because it was found to be the only right and equitable way for all the members of the society to tread upon for peaceful living. It has been popularly called dharma, not just religion, nor creed, nor duty in the westerner's sense. It was the whole conduct of the individual in his personal, social and national life. It was the central principle that guided him and all members of the society so that the society, as a whole, could function in peace and tranquility. The main idea behind the principle was that all members of the society keep an ideal, a standard of conduct, or a restraining line - a sort of "Lakshman Rekha" which, if crossed, was fraught with problems, pain and sufferings such as was experienced by Sita as shown in the Ramayana. This principle is similar to or part of the idea which the Vedic poet called Rita or right conduct. Max Muller calls this the Third Beyond and explains it thus:

"But there is still another Beyond (guide) that found expression in the ancient religion of India. Besides the devas or the gods and besides the pitris or fathers, there was a third world without which the ancient religion of India could not have become what we see it in the Veda. That third beyond was what the poets of the Veda call the Rita, and which I believe meant originally no more than the `straight line'. It is applied to the straight line of the sun in its daily course, to the straight line followed by day and night, to the straight line that regulates the seasons, to the straight line which, in spite of many momentary deviations, was discovered to run through the whole realm of nature. We call that Rita, that straight or right line, when we apply it in a more general sense, the Law of Nature; and when we apply it to the moral world, we try to express the same idea again by speaking of the Moral Law, the law on which our life is founded, the eternal Law of

Right and Reason..."[2]

The essence of the Vedic religion or the Hindu way has been the right conduct which is commonly known as dharma. This is the ultimate principle which is hammered into the Hindu mind by all the great men age after age and followed or obeyed in more or less measure by all members of the Hindu society as if it is the command of their respective deities. Conforming to the essentials of its resource - the Veda, including the Buddhist teachings, and those of other smaller sects or panths, which emanated from the same resourace, insist upon the practice of the same Hindu virtues when they make their familiar invocation like "dharamam sharanam gachhami" in order to find ultimate peace in the dharma.

Thus the values or the commandments prescribed in the Vedic literature (the beyonds or guides) are the safety devices and defences for human society. Through these guidelines the "men and gods collaborated to keep the universe operating smoothly and thwart the machinations of demons and their misguided allies."[3]

RIGHT CONDUCT:

(THE GUIDE FOR RIGHTEOUSNESS IS YOUR OWN MANAH (FREE MIND).

---

[2] Max Muller, The Vedas, p. 145

[3] W. Norman Brown, Mythology of India, p. 281

IDEAL HUMANS ELEVATED TO DIVINE STATUS

THE GOAL

"Professor Garbe, who devoted a large part of his life to the study of the Sankhya, consoled himself with the thought that `in Kapila's doctrine, for the first time in the history of the world, the complete independence and freedom of the human mind, its full confidence in its own powers, were exhibited."[1] Hinduism is freedom, especially the freedom in thinking about God. In search of the supernatural, it is like travelling in space without a boundary or barrier. Liberation from the cycle of rebirth or union of the individual soul with the Supreme Soul, Absolute Brahman, is the goal of all Hindu thought. Without denying the agnostics and atheists their rights, and to the man in the street his materialistic objectives, the ultimate goal of a Hindu seeker is "moksha". liberation or freedom from the cycle of coming in and going from this world so that it can merge into or find communion with the Supreme Soul - the Universality, the Eternity, the Infinity, the beginning less and endless Existence beyond the barriers of time and space. "When the self realizes that it is free from all contacts with nature, it is released."[2] All Indian sages and seers have had just this ceaseless passion for freeing the soul from the continuing bondage of and suffering from maya. And only those can feel the pain of this bondage who have known the suffering of chains. As per Will Durant, the last word of Hindu religious thought is moksha, release - first from desire, then from life. "Salvation does not come by faith, nor yet by works; it comes by such uninterrupted self-denial, by such selfless intuition of the part engulfing whole, that at last the self is dead, and there is nothing to be born. The hell of individuality passes into the haven and heaven of unity, of complete and impersonal absorption into

---

[1] Will Durant, Our Oriental Heritage, p. 536
[2] S. Radhakrishnan, Bhagvadgita, p. 55

Brahman, the soul or force of the world."[3]

Moksha or nirvana implies freedom first from desire and then from the bondage of `awagaman' the birth and death cycle of the entrapped soul. Freedom from desire makes way for the freedom from the cycle of birth and death. This bondage is broken through perfection of the soul by pursuit of jnana (wisdom), unselfish works, or by devotion to God or by whatever other method that may suit the seeker, wherein detachment from attachment to materialistic living becomes the means or the end or both. In the process, the seeker abjures desire which causes attachment and bondage. The man thus liberated, has passed from the sphere of karma, `action', into the sphere of jnana (transcendent wisdom), omniscience, which is synonymous with all knowledgeable state, Parmeshwar, Brahman. Works can never bind him, for he is wholly detached from them. They find their culmination in wisdom where after nothing remains to be done or undone. His is a state of being where there is no individuality left. He sees All in himself and himself in all things. For him all is One in essence though they appear diverse; and there is neither earth, nor water, nor fire nor air, neither sun, nor moon, neither this world, nor the next, nor heaven, nor hell. There is neither coming nor going, nor standing still, nor falling, nor rising: it is all Existence, here and beyond and in eternity.

In the pursuit of moksha Hinduism does not prescribe just faith in any one person or prophet for the guidance. It aims at realization through perfection of the self by nishkam karmas (unselfish works). It is at once scientific or reasonable. According to Romain Rolland,

---

[3] Will Durant, <u>Our Oriental Heritage</u>, p. 517

"Religious faith in the case of Indians has never been allowed to run counter to scientific laws, moreover the former is never made a condition for the knowledge they teach; but they are always scrupulously careful to take into consideration the possibility that by reason both the agnostic and the atheist may attain truth in their own way. Such tolerance may be surprising to religious believers in the West, but it is an integral part of Vedantic belief.[4] The goal is not to find God, a god, the heaven, a kingdom of God on earth, permanent youthfulness or eternal life; but it is the abolishment of individual identity for merger into the Ultimate.

Philosophically, Hinduism accepts no dogma, no laws, no rules, no rites or rituals and no requirement of temple or place of worship. Yet like any other religion, it has the structure - the temples with or without idols, the rules, the rituals and the worship of God that the common man needs for his psychological security. It has even the misused and abused `Swastika' as a sign of welfare painted on the orthodox Hindu homes. And the `Star of David' must be drawn by most Hindu priests to build an altar for lighting the yajna (sacrificial) fire. In this way, "Hindus swallow all religions into the great body of Hinduism, e.g., Vedanta embraces all scriptures of the world." [5] This unique way of God worship, which theoretically requires no statues, no pictures or posters, no dance or drama, and which needs no temples or teachers or gurus or incarnations, helpful though they all are, but only the freedom of mind of the worshipper, is born out of free thinking minds of the Hindu seers and saints whose only obsession was freedom here and freedom

---

[4] Romain Rolland, Life and Gospel of Vivekanands, p. 229

[5] Swami Abhedananda, The Path of Realization, p.5

hereafter without which nothing had any value. "Das wesen des geistes is die freiheit" (The essence of the spirit is liberty), as Hegel said.

Pursuit for liberation through jnana, karma or abstract meditation has been the ideal method for Hindu seers and philosophers; but the common man has been doing the traditional worship of God through the worship of His incarnations or lesser manifestations of His powers such as the sun, the moon, the wind, the fire, the water, and other objects of nature, or other worthy beings such as the father, the mother, the teacher, the preacher, the cow, or any other living being, directly or through pictures or statues. No one form of worship is recommended. It can be by sitting, standing, prostrating, sleeping, singing, dancing, fasting, feasting, doing, or not doing, or even by doubting His existence as Buddha did.

TRUTH - SAT, CHIT, ANANDA:

TRUTH POSTULATES KNOWLEDGE (CIT); AND THE TRUE KNOWLEDGE BRINGS ABOUT BLISS (ANANDA).

THE LOWER GOALS
Gods and Goddesses

Lower goals by pleasing one or many gods, the functionaries of supernatural powers of creation, preservation and destruction such as Brahma, Vishnu and Mahesh respectively, and a host of other lower gods manifesting nature such as sun, moon, air, fire, etc., are objects of worship of common people needing worldly welfare like health, happiness, name, fame, material wealth, beautiful spouse, children, long life, etc. So people in full freedom are entitled to worship and work for whatever immediate or ultimate goal they want to reach. Hinduism appreciates these pursuits for whatever worth they are. Vinoba Bhave says: "The worldly people also do much penance; but it is in pursuit of low aims. We reap what we sow; as is the desire, so is the fruit. The world will not pay more for our wares than the price we ourselves mark on them."[1] "The Supreme Lord of the Gita confirms the faith of each and grants the rewards each seeks . . . No matter what we revere, so long as our reverence is serious, it helps progress."[2] "Those devoted to perfected saints (or the ancestors) will go to them, worshippers of ghosts will go to the ghosts."[3]

By the force of their nature or inclination of their personalities evolved and developed and conditioned through their karmas (works) in previous births and the environment of the existing lives, most people are normally inclined to worship smaller gods for smaller worldly gains or for short-lived pleasures even on earth and in heaven. These benefits and pleasures are not permanent. Therefore, on expiration of the tenure

---

[1] Vinoba Bhave, Talks on the Gita, p. 30
[2] S. Radhakrishnan, Bhagvadgita, p. 222
[3] R. C. Zaehner, The Bhagvadgita, notes on p. 253

of their good deeds, these people have to return to the earth or are born again and again to resume their unfinished (karmas) for ongoing quest for the liberation of their souls. The following shlokas from the Gita confirm this view:

> 7.21[1] yo yo yam yam tanum bhaktah sraddhaya 'rcitum icchati,
> tasya tasy'acalam
> sraddham tam eva vidadhamyaham.

Meaning: Whichever god a devotee desires to worship with faith, I confirm in him that very faith in accordance with his nature and instinct. (Herein the Hindu thought allows freedom not to have even the best if one doesn't want the best.)

> 7.23[2] antavat tu phalam tesam tad bhavaty alpamedhasam;
> devan deva-yajo yanti, mad-bbakta
> yanti mam api.

Meaning: Men of limited knowledge have limited and temporary reward. Such persons do reach whatever smaller gods they worship, but he who worships Me will come to me indeed regardless of his manner of worship.

---

[1] यो यो यां यां तनुं भक्तः श्रद्धयार्चितुमिच्छति ।
तस्य तस्याचलां श्रद्धां तामेव विदधाम्यहम् ॥

[2] अन्तवत्तु फलं तेषां तद्भवत्यल्पमेधसाम् ।
देवान्देवयजो यान्ति मद्भक्ता यान्ति मामपि ॥

9.20[1] traividya mam soma-pah puta-papa
yajnair istva svar-gatim prartheyante
te punyam asadya sur'endra-lokam
asnanti diivyan divi deva-bhogan.

Meaning: The som drinkers, after being cleansed of their sins and with belief in three vedas, worship Me with sacrifice seeking to reach heaven. These persons, do attain to heaven and enjoy their gods' celestial pleasures as a result of their good deeds.

9.21[2] te tam huktva svarga-lokam visalam ksine punye martya-lokam visanti; vam trayi-dharmam anuprapanna
gat'agatam kama-kama labhante.

Meaning: These people, on exhausting their accumulated good deeds through enjoyment of the grandeur of the vast paradise, return to the world of humans. Therefore, persons aspiring heaven for gratification of their desires have to move up and down time and again.

For more information see shlokas 23 and 25 in chapter 9, and shlokas 1 and 4 in chapter 17.

There are two types of worshippers in this world. Those who truly and sincerely seek union with God, and those who, incidentally desire to see God, but actually want the fulfillment of their

---

[1] त्रैविद्या मां सोमपाः पूतपापा
यज्ञैरिष्ट्वा स्वर्गतिं प्रार्थयन्ते ।
[2] ते पुण्यमासाद्य सुरेन्द्रलोक-
मश्नन्ति दिव्यान्दिवि देवभोगान् ॥

ते तं भुक्त्वा स्वर्गलोकं विशालं
क्षीणे पुण्ये मर्त्यलोकं विशन्ति ।
एवं त्रयीधर्ममनुप्रपन्ना
गतागतं कामकामा लभन्ते ॥

worldly desires by doing rituals and pleasing lower gods. In the above verses the teacher "refers to the Vedic theory that those who perform the prescribed rituals do gain even heaven after death and points out how even heaven cannot be regarded as the highest goal. All men are bound by the law of karma which, good or bad, bind the doer. When they worship their god with desire (kama-kamah) for worldly gains, they do get their cherished material objects: wealth, health, lovely homes, beautiful or handsome spouse, children, power, position , or whatever they wished for; but after exhausting their merit in heaven, they have to return to this world as they act from an ego-center and their ignorance is not destroyed.

WORK AND WORSHIP
(NOT FAITH ALONE)

Work without attachment or a spiritual exercise to perfect, condition, and integrate the soul into the Supreme Soul is the basis for attaining liberation (moksha) as against mere believing. Hindu thought has not taken for granted without verification the word of any saint, seer, a messenger of God, a son of God or an incarnation of God. It has gone all out to realize Him and see Him face to face. And truthful as the Hindu devotees were in their quest, they were not only revered but worshipped because those having realized the Ultimate had become one with Him. Realization, therefore, presupposes effort. Without work (karma sadhna) for perfection, there is no progress toward the goal, be it for a lessor god, or the heaven or the Ultimate Being. Just mercy or grace without work (karma) does not help. A simple `faithful' doesn't get moksha or God in Hinduism. Troy Organ calls it a process for perfection: "Hinduism is a sadhna which seeks to guide man to integration, to spiritualism, and to liberation . . . . It is a process, not a result - a process of perfecting man."[1] There is, however, not just one process in Hinduism. Many processes were systematized, but the most important of them all are the six systems of Hindu philosophy mentioned earlier. Added to them are the philosophies, rules and rituals of other important religions like Buddhism, Jainism and several other sects. And the people have the freedom to worship a god, a guru, an incarnation, or the Ultimate Being of whatever name, and in whatever manner.

Study of the vedas, the shastras, the puranas, the Bhagvadgita and the epics, etc. scriptures, are, in fact, the means to the end. Hinduism recognizes the value of the scriptures and the teacher (guru) only to guide and help the devotee in his yoga, sadhna or worship of

---

[1] Troy Wilson Organ, The Hindu Quest for the Perfection of Man, p. 5

God. A master teacher's role is considered a bit higher than most religious books because at best he is knowledge personified; he alone can answer questions and remove doubts of the devotee. But once the devotee has reached the stage of perfection, he needs none of the `help books' as he has already become one with the Supreme. Therefore, those who have attained real knowledge have no need for the scriptures.

Shrimad Bhagvadgita does not take away from the humans their right to reach Brahm or become one with God. Any person who has perfected himself is as good as a book of religion in Hinduism. In other words, the scriptures cannot surpass the perfected person who has become one with God. The poet refers to the institution of the real Guru with supernatural powers who is known to his disciples capable of performing miracles or unnatural things in unusual circumstances. Incarnations of God needed no books!

Ramakrishna Paramhamsa, not very long ago, has taught the world that religion is a matter not so much of believing but of experience which has been the traditional Hindu way. He was a man without a college education and proved to the world that formal academic education was not a prerequisite to the attainment of spirituality. Paying tribute to him in 1908, Shri Aurobindo wrote:

"In Bengal there came a flood of religious truth. Certain men were born, men whom the educated world would not have recognized if that belief, if that God within them, had not been there to open their eyes, men whose lives were very different from what our education, our Western education, taught us to admire. One of them, the man who had the greatest influence and has done the most to regenerate Bengal, could not read and write a single word. He was a man who had been what they call absolutely useless to the world. But he had this one divine faculty in him, that he had more than faith and had realized God . . . . He was a man without intellectual training . . . . But God knew what he was doing. He sent that man to Bengal and set him in the temple of Dakshineshwar in Calcutta, and from North and South and East and West, the educated men, men who were the pride of the University, who had studied all that Europe can teach, came to fall at the feet of this ascetic. The work of salvation, the work of raising India was begun."[1]

Every country and certainly India abounds in persons who had no formal schooling or education in religion and yet they are known to have realized God. The names of Surdas, Meera, Kabir, Nanak, Dadu, Tukaram, etc. of the modern times, are household words in bhakti inspiring one and all with the ecstasy of their devotional songs. Despite the fact that their religion was desecrated and their people butchered, persecuted, and robbed of their possessions and political power by invading barbarians, these saints preached tolerance, acceptance, and love for all alike. This Hindu tradition of love for all alike did not stop even when they were ultimately masters of their own land, as under their great leader Mahatma Gandhi, they showed to the world that they still could tolerate and accept in their country, differences based on religion.

As love and respect has been the basis for social relationship, use of force against the enemy has been resorted to in extreme circumstances when they were left with no other choice. The philosophers did recommend the use of force discarding their love of non-violence. The rationale being that the goodness is just not to be acquired but protected by force. Lord Krishna's famous quotation in the

---

[1] A.B. Purani, Sri Aurobindo, p.38

Gita that in times of real need He Himself incarnates in this world to protect the good ones, has been an authority from ancient times:

4.7[1] yada yada he dharmasya glanir bhavati, Bharata, abhyutthanam adharmasya tada'tmanam srjamy aham.

Meaning: Whenever the law of righteousness declines, and the lawlessness develops, O Arjuna, then I appear myself on this earth.

4.8[2] paritranaya sadhunam vinasaya ca duskrtam, dharma-samsthapan'arthaya sambhavami yuge yuge.

Meaning: For the protection of the good people, for the destruction of the evildoers, and for the rehabilitation of righteousness, I manifest myself age after age.

God worship in Hinduism is not just chanting prayers, going to temples or doing rituals. It involves social responsibilities and imposes political obligations. If it was just to do the idle praying, Lord Krishna wouldn't have advised Pandavs to fight the bloodiest civil war at Kurukshetra and Rama wouldn't be fighting Ravana to punish him for his wrongs. In essence, God worship in Hinduism enjoins effort, work, and sadhna along with faith and prayers. Work is worship from which He Himself is not immune since symbolizing Him, the entire cosmos, as a single unified entity, is working continuously, tirelessly and regularly like His tiny incarnate, the honey bee. Man has discretion. In his freedom, he gets wayward and is lured into dualities (maya) so he gets attached

---

[1] यदा यदा हि धर्मस्य ग्लानिर्भवति भारत ।
अभ्युत्थानमधर्मस्य तदात्मानं सृजाम्यहम् ॥

[2] परित्राणाय साधूनां विनाशाय च दुष्कृताम् ।
धर्मसंस्थापनार्थाय संभवामि युगे युगे ॥

to the fruits of his action making his goal blurred; but once, through yoga, he attains discrimination and clear thinking, he is liberated. Shrimad Bhagvadgita glorifies the working man who has renounced the fruits of his actions:

3.9[1] yajn'arthat karmano 'nyatra loko 'yam
karma-bandhanah:
tad-artham karma, Kaunteya,
muktasangah-samacara.

Meaning: This world is bound by work except where the work is done for sacrifice. If you work as a sacrifice, then O Arjuna, you will be liberated.

6.46[2] tapasvibhyo'dhika yogi jnanibhyo'pi
mato'dhikah,
karmibhyas c'adhiko yogi;
tasmad yogi bhav'arjuna.

Meaning: Higher than the ascetic is the man who works without attachment to the fruits. He is higher than the man of knowledge and he is, of course, higher than the man working for the fruits. Therefore, O Arjuna, be a karmayogi unattached to the fruits.

Yoga may be understood to be a system entirely independent of jnana (theory). In yoga opposite do not exclude, but complement each

---

1 यज्ञार्थात्कर्मणोऽन्यत्र लोकोऽयं कर्मबन्धनः ।
   तदर्थं कर्म कौन्तेय मुक्तसङ्गः समाचर ॥

2 तपस्विभ्योऽधिको योगी ज्ञानिभ्योऽपि मतोऽधिकः ।
   कर्मिभ्यश्चाधिको योगी तस्माद्योगी भवार्जुन ॥

works, his unselfish actions remain the vehicle to carry him close to God. Knowledge and meditation together with selfless works culminate into Wisdom (jnana), the ultimate estate which is necessarily the cessation of all actions. This integrated state, according to the verse 6.47 of the Gita, is the basis for ultimate union with God and is possible only to those who are already integrated, purified and liberated.

WORSHIP WITHOUT WORK IS LIKE CHEATING OTHERS AND FOOLING GOD WHO HIMSELF WORKS ETERNALLY.

PARAMATMA, BRAHMAN
(GOD OR WHATEVER)

Vedas and Hindu seers have been honest in describing Him. He is Being (sat - eternal being), and Not-Being (asat - conditioned or contingent being). He is not knowable. Thomas Paine said: "The only idea man can affix to the name of God is ... at the belief of it from the tenfold greater difficulty of disbelieving it."[1] But the Jain prophet Mahabira thought it fit to disbelieve Him outrightly. Buddha likewise did not indulge into the controversy, unending as it is, and stayed doubtful; but went straight into requiring humans to perfect themselves through noble deeds and non-violence for peace and nirvana. True seers and saints all over the world are unanimous in giving no precise description of Him. Radhakrishnan says: "Strictly speaking, we cannot give any description of Brahman. The austerity of silence is the only way in which we can bring out the inadequacy of our halting descriptions and imperfect standards . . . . The eternal one is so infinitely real that we dare not even give It the name of One since oneness is an idea derived from worldly experience . . . The Upanishads indulge in negative account, that the Real is not this, not this (ne iti, ne iti)"[2] St. Augustine says: "We can know what God is not, but cannot know what He is."[3]

Still for our limited faculties, space and time serve two quite obvious manifestations of eternity - the Ultimate Realty "as it is universal Here, so is it an everlasting Now."[4]

Thus some say His form is the entire Creation - space, billions and billions of solar systems and regions beyond where human thinking

---

[1] Thomas Paine, The Age of Reason - I, p. 1794
[2] S. Radhakrishnan, Bhagvadgita, p. 21
[3] St. Augustine: De trinitate.
[4] Thomas Carlyle, Sarter Resartus, iii

cannot reach; and it has all the things on earth from molecule to mountain, from ant to elephant and then the humans, the most perfect of the living beings - good and bad, saints and scoundrels included. Likewise his age is the Time, the time eternal. Time, moving forward, never backward, is the base of the universe on which all else rests in reality. He has no beginning and no end which means, He never was born and He is never going to die. He has no size, no shape, no color and, infact, no attribute whatsoever. He can be any one of all the things in the world or all of them together, or nothing at all. The same uncertainty is expressed by Kant "There is, and is not, an absolutely necessary Being."[1]

A very interesting description is given of Him in the Brihad Aranyaka[2] in the famous dialogue between the great sage Yajnavalkya and a woman philosopher Gargi who was earlier warned by the sage not to ask such questions:

"She said: `That, O Yajnavalkya, which is above the sky, that which is beneath the earth, that which is between these two, sky and earth, that which people call the past and the present and the future - across what is that woven, warp and woof?'

He said: `That, O Gargi, which is above the sky, that which is beneath the earth, that which is between these two, sky and earth, that which people call the past and the present and the future - across space is that woven, warp, and woof.'

She said: `Adoration to you, Yajnavalkya, in that you solved this question for me. Prepare yourself for the other.'

---

1. Immanuel Kant, quoted from Bertrand Russell,
   History of Western Philosophy, p. 709
2. Brihad Aranyaka, III: 82-12, in Hume, The Thirteen

'Ask Gargi.'

She said: 'That, O Yajnavalkya, which is above the sky, that which is beneath the earth, that which is between these two, sky and earth, that which people call the past and the present and the future - across what is that woven, warp and woof?'

He said: 'That, O Gargi, which is above the sky, that which is beneath the earth, that which is between these two, sky and earth, that which people call the past and the present and the future - across space alone is that woven, warp and woof.'

'Across what then, pray, is space woven, warp and woof?'

He said: 'That, O Gargi, Brahman call the Imperishable (aksara). It is not course, not fine, not short, not long, not glowing, not adhesive, without shadow and without darkness, without air and without space, without stickiness (intangible), odorless, tasteless, without eye, without ear, without voice, without wind, without energy, without breath, without mouth, (without personal or family name, unaging, undying, without fear, immortal, stainless, not uncovered, not covered), without measure, without inside and without outside.

> It consumes nothing soever
> No one soever consumes it.

Verily, O Gargi, at the command of that imperishable the sun and the moon stand apart. Verily, O Gargi, at the command of that Imperishable the earth and the sky stand apart. Verily, O Gargi, at the command of that Imperishable the moments, the hours, the days, the nights, the fortnights, the months, the seasons and the years stand apart. Verily, O Gargi, at the command of that Imperishable some rivers flow from the snowy mountains to the east, others to the west, in whatever direction each flows. Verily, O Gargi, at the command of that Imperishable men praise those who give, the gods are desirous of a sacrificer, and the fathers are desirous of the Manes-sacrifice. Verily, O Gargi, if one performs sacrifices and worship and undergoes austerity in this world for many thousands of years, but without knowing that Imperishable, limited indeed is that work of his. Verily, O Gargi, he who departs from this world without knowing that Imperishable is pitiable. But, O Gargi, he who departs from this world knowing that Imperishable is Brahman.

Verily, O Gargi, that Imperishable is the unseen Seer, the unheard Hearer, the unthought Thinker, the ununderstood Understander. Other than It there is naught that sees. Other than It there is naught that hears. Other than It there is naught that thinks. Other than It there is naught that understands. Across this Imperishable, O Gargi, is space woven, warp and woof.'

She said: 'Venerable Brahman, you may think it is a great thing you may escape from this man with merely making a bow. Not one of you will surpass him in discussions about Brahman.' Thereupon Gargi held her peace!"

This confusion is aptly described in Isa Upanishad (9-10) thus:

> Blind darkness enter they
> Who revere the uncompounded.
> Into a darkness blinder yet
> (Go they) who delight in the compounded.
> Other, they say, then what becomes,
> Other, they say, that what does not

become:
So from wise men have we heard
Who instructed us therein.

He is untraceable and unreachable. In Kathopnishad (6.7-8) He is described as the highest Person beyond everything else but without any trace:

> Higher than the senses is the mind,
> Higher than the mind, the soul (sattava),
> Higher than the soul, the self, the `great',
> Higher than the 'great, the 'Unmanifest',
> Higher than the 'Unmanifest', the
> `Person', (Purusa),Pervadingall,untraceable.

But without laying claim to philosophy, the great English poet Alexander Pope gives a beautiful portrayal of Him in this easy-to-understand metaphor:

> "All are but parts of one stupendous whole,
> Whose body nature is, and God the soul."[1]

---

[1] Alexander Pope in <u>An Essay on Man</u>

He is pure consciousness: The soul looking through human body's senses perceives this universe transformed as earth, stars, planets sky, suns, moons, oceans and mountains which though stupendous looking are nothing in measurement to what the soul looks at the same spectacle unhampered by the senses when "hard boundaries melt and fade revealing pure consciousness as the sovereign reality behind the diversity of the sense-created universe." [1]

Such spectacles can be seen only by a spiritual exercise in the process of sadhna when the soul breaks out of the bodily boundaries and looks directly into what this author had experienced some fifty one years ago when his own soul was lost in the Universe and he saw nothing but space or the void all around. Being not very much developed spiritually to sustain the impact of that vision, he certainly remembers being scared in the afloat condition, and promptly forced himself to return to his normal self. He is not ashamed to admit that never again did he venture to go back into smadhi; but after having personally experienced the phenomena, he is more than ever convinced that the formations of billions of the objects of nature in the space will appear vanished when seen directly by the soul. Chapter XI of Shrimad Bhagvadgita describes this consciousness in detail. Here is how Arjuna describes Parmatma after seeing His Virat Roop (Krishna's transfiguration) before the beginning of the War at Kurukshetra:

> dyavaprathivyor idam anataram hi
> vyaptam tvayai 'kena disas ca sarvah
> drstva 'dbhutam rupam ugram tave 'dam
> lokatrayam pravyathitam mahatman

Meaning: This space between heaven and earth is pervaded by Thee

---

[1] Gene Kieffer, <u>Kundalini Empowering Human Evolution,</u> p. 299

alone; and on seeing this wondrous terrible form of Thine, all the directions of the sky and the three worlds tremble with fear!

11.30[1] lelihyase grasamanah samantal
lokan samagran vadanair jvaladbhih
tejobhir apurya jagat samagram
bhasas tavo 'grah pratapaanti visno

Meaning: devouring all the worlds with Thy flaming mouths, thou licks them up; and O Vishnu, Thy fiery rays fill and scorch this whole universe with their fierce radiance. **And Krishna tells Arjuna to see for himself what He is; and so he must do what He tells him to do in this war of righteousness:**

11.7[2] ih'aika-stham jagat krtsnam
pasy'adya sacar'acaram
mama dehe, Gudakesa,
yacc'anyad drastum icchasi.

Meaning: O Arjuna, look in this body of mine, centered at one place, the entire creation both animate and inanimate and all other things that you want to see.

11.33[3] tasmat tvam uttistha, yaso labhasva,
jitva satrun bhunksva rajyam samrddham:
may'aiv'aite nihatah purvam eva:
nimitta-matram bhava, savya-sacin.

---

1 लेलिह्यसे ग्रसमानः समन्ता- ल्लोकान्समग्रान्वदनैर्ज्वलद्भिः ।
   तेजोभिरापूर्य्यं जगत्समग्रं भासस्तवोग्राः प्रतपन्ति विष्णो ॥

2 इहैकस्थं जगत्कृत्स्नं पश्याद्य सचराचरम् । मम देहे गुडाकेश यच्चान्यद्द्रष्टुमिच्छसि ॥

3 तस्मान्त्वमुत्तिष्ठ यशो लभस्व जित्वा शत्रून्भुङ्क्ष्व राज्यं समृद्धम् ।
   मयैवैते निहताः पूर्वमेव निमित्तमात्रं भव सव्यसाचिन् ॥

Meaning: And so get up, win glory, and a prosperous kingdom by conquering your adversaries. Long since have they been slain by Me: yours will be the mere occasion.

Personal God or Impersonal Absolute

Fools have been arguing this and barbarians have used the so called difference in the two modes of worship for religious wars, inquisitions, persecutions, wholesale exterminations, and an excuse for proselytizing innocent `infidels.' They robbed, raped and enslaved in thousands men and women belonging to other religions. Even now when we are at the threshold of the twenty first century, most people are as bigot, fanatic or racist as they were in the dark ages.

Even though image worship, being unknown to Aryan Hindus before Buddha around 6th century B.C., and was imported from Greece, there is a rationale behind the idol worship. Therefore, both modes of worship are right, as in both, the worshipper, unless he is a rare abstract thinker, has to have some kind of image of the object of worship whether it is statue, or a sign, or an imaginative conception of the god he worships. Hindu saints have personally realized the Supreme Being in whatever form they wanted Him to see, and brought His manifestation, Krishna, Rama, Shiva, Hanuman, Mother Kali, or any other deity, face to face with themselves. Serving and worshipping God in human form is common man's puja or bhakti. It is the worship of a personal god where the god or less powerful deity or object is given a symbolic form for his attributes; and through the image or the picture of the deity, the worshipper tries to find oneness with the deity symbolized in the image or the picture. The deity is close for the devotee's security and the deity's personal service by the devotee. "The saguna engages the mind and the senses....In saguna, the eyes can see the Lord's form, the ears can hear His praises, the hands can offer worship to Him and serve human beings in His various forms."[1] "Worship of the personal god is recommended as the easier way open to all, the weak and the lowly, the illiterate and the ignorant."[2] But this form of worship has found expression in the greatest of the intellectuals. The poet Tulsidas of India, the author of the Ramayana, which is as popular in north Indian Hindus as the Bible in Christians, was one such person who worshipped his god in human form whom he is believed to have met in person.

The concept of personal and impersonal aspects of God (Brahman), popularly known as Saguna and Nirguna respectively, rests on the supposition whether God is with attributes or without attributes. When Brahman is supposed to be conditioned by His own maya and given a form or anthropomorphic personality, He is known as saguna Brahman or Isvara; but when Brahman is said to be devoid of qualifying charateristics so that He cannot be pointed out or described by any sign, then He is called nirguna Brahman. The first is upheld by those who regard the world as real and God its Creater, Sustainer and Destroyer. But according to the other view, the world of names and forms is finally unreal and transient. All that is perceived anywhere is Brahman alone in totality. In that case all elements are alike, parts of the One Whole, God. "Aham Brahmosmi", so says Jagadguru Shankracharya to proclaim the essential Unity of the apparent multiplicity. In this context He is nirguna Brahman. The entire universe is filled with Him. There is nothing superior to Him, and none equal to Him. He ALONE is the totality.

It is hard to separate the two kinds of worship as both are essentially the same. The difference lies in the initial approach. In saguna bhakti, for instance, the bhakta has the structure, the symbol,

---

[1] Acharya Vinoba Bhave, Talks on the Gita , p.64
[2] S. Radhakrishnan, Bhagvadgita, p.64

most of the time, right in front of him. He can have the deity, object of his worship present in person like Lakshmana had in Rama when he looked after him day in and day out. His prayer (puja) consisted of complete service to his God whom he perceived in Rama. He had no need for any scriptures or temples. This was obvious when he was discouraged from accompanying Rama in exile and he simply got nerve-broken saying that without Rama he wouldn't live. On the other hand, we find in Bharat an ideal nirguna upasak of the Lord. Bharat too loved Rama as much as Lakshmana did; but as he had to perform his task of governing the kingdom, he could ill afford the luxury of saguna upasana. Hence, he had to be content with serving the Lord from a distance keeping his image in his heart. The nirguna upasak, as some may misunderstand, does not eliminate all symbols of God or Absolute Being from his mind even for a moment. He keeps Him within and is engaged in doing His work like Bharat did. The difference thus lies in the object being far or near to the worshipper for his security. His objective can be sagun or nirgun upasana. "There is no difference between sagun and nirgun as per vedas, puranas, munis and the learned. The abstract Unmanifest becomes manifest out of love for His devotees."[1]

Nirguna, more than saguna, has been the way of philosophy. The practice can be through Jnana (Sankhya) Yoga or Raja Yoga in which the yogi engages in abstract contemplation and meditation. His guides usually are scriptures, especially Upanishads and Shastras, that take him toward his destination step by step. These Hindu shashtras are scientific explanations employing logic, reason and rationality developed by practicing saints and seers with positive results over the centuries. "No one of these yogas gives up reason, no one of them asks you to be hoodwinked or deliver your reasons into the hands of priests of any type whatsoever .... Each one of them tells you to cling to your

---

[1] Goswami Tulsidas, Ramcharitmanas, Balkand, 16.1

सगुनहि अगुनहि नहिं कछु भेदा ✻ गावहिं मुनि पुरान बुध बेदा
अगुन अरूप अलख अज जोई ✻ भगत प्रेम बस सगुन सो होई

reason, to hold fast to it."[2]

God does not care whether one worships Him in human form or as an impersonal Absolute. He is like this mother who had two sons. One was a few years older than the other. The younger son who was not yet quite big to be left alone was always attached to the mother who gave him more attention; but the older boy who now went to school had to be left alone for some time as he felt no physical need for the mother although he too remembered her and felt her absence. Now between the two of them, the mother was asked whom she loved more. The mother was in a dilemma. She loved her both sons equally although she did hug the younger son closely because he was younger and less mature than the older. She could afford to miss the older boy for a while as he was more understanding. In this context a question was addressed to Lord Krishna by Arjuna during the course of the Lecture on the battlefield in Kurukshetra. The question in 1.2 of the Gita is:

"Of those who are thus very integrated and serve you with devotion, and those who meditate on imperishable Unmanifest, which are the most developed?"

The Lord God Krishna answered him thus in 12.2 thru 12.12 of the Gita:

Those who fix their thoughts on Me as Personal God and serve Me with full devotion and perfection and their minds fully integrated are lifted up right soon into joining Me. But those who do abstract thinking and meditate on the Impersonal, Absolute Being, who hold in check their

---

[2] Romain Rolland, <u>The Life and Gospel of Vivekananda,</u> p. 235

senses, and are in all things equal minded, staying same in all dualities, they too attain to Me as I am available to both kinds.

Thus no one way is better than the other in reaching Him. Whoever with love and devotion worships Him comes to Him. It does not matter whether you employ the head or the heart in devotion. The essence of the whole exercise lies in the truth and sincerity and the effort employed in the worship.

Yet Hindu saints and seers have been arguing the nature and form of God philosophically. Two main currents, known as Dvaitvad and Advaitvad (dualism and non-dualism), have dominated their thinking. Dvaitvad, modified by the 11th century philosopher Ramanujacharya, as Vishistadvaitvad, establishes the phenomenal world alongside the world of spirits.

Radhakrishnan's explanation of his philosophy of Vishistadvaitvad is this: "...The world and God are one as body and soul are one. They are a whole but at the same time unchangeably different. Before creation, the world is in a potential form, undeveloped into the existing and diversified manifestations. In creation, it is developed into name and form (namarupa). By representing the world as the body of God, it is suggested that the world is not made from something alien, a second principle, but is produced by the Supreme out of His own nature. God is both the instrumental and the material cause of the world. This analogy is used to indicate the absolute dependence of the world on God even as the body is absolutely dependent on the soul. The world is not only the body of God but His remainder, `isvarasyasesa', and this phrase suggests the complete dependence and contingency of the world.

"...Ramanuja develops in his commentary on the Gita a type of personal mysticism. In the secret places of the human soul, God dwells but He is unrecognized by it so long as the soul does not acquire the redeeming knowledge. We acquire this knowledge by serving God with our whole heart and soul."

"...The Supreme is Visnu, for Ramanuja. He is the only true god who will not share His divine honors with others. Liberation is service of and fellowship with God in Vaikuntha or heaven."[1]

Samkara (A.D. 788-820) is the greatest exponent of Advaitvad or non-dualistic theory of God since the Medieval period. Radhakrishnan interprets him thus: "...Samkara affirms that Reality or Brahman is one without a second. The entire world of manifestation and multiplicity is not real in itself and seems to be real only for those who live in ignorance (avidya). To be caught in it is the bondage in which we are all implicated. This lost condition cannot be removed by our efforts. Works are vain and bind us firmly to this unreal cosmic process (samsara), the endless chain of cause and effect. Only the wisdom that the universal reality and the individual self are identical can bring us redemption. When this wisdom arises, the ego is dissolved, the wandering ceases and we have perfect joy and blessedness."[2]

Interpreting Chandogya Upanishad (6.1.4) R.C. Zaehner says this about non-dualism: "Just as all that is made up of clay can be known by one lump of clay - its modifications are verbalizations, (mere) names - its reality is just `clayness'; so is what IS."[3] And Will Durant comments upon Samkara's non-dualism as follows: "Such a deity, says this pre-plagiarist of Kant, cannot be proved by reason, he can only be postulated as a practical necessity, offering to our limited intellects and

---

[1] Radhakrishnan, <u>Bhagvadgita,</u> p.18-19
[2] Ibid, p. 17
[3] R.C. Zaehner, <u>The Bhagvadgita, </u>p.8

encouragement to our fragile morality...."[1]

To put it differently, all diversity and multiplicity is unfractionably one single entity; and all that we see around and also what we are disabled from seeing due to our limited powers is what is real Existence, Truth, Unity, Supreme Soul or God. God is nothing but transcendental reality of which material universe is only a manifestation. Individual self and universal self appear different to those unenlightened persons who cannot see beyond their environment or individual selves. In fact, and in essence, seemingly different selves are basically one and the same thing. The difference arose due to the data presented by the senses. But as soon as a person gets realization or knowledge, he is able to see clearly into the
illusions of matter; he is integrated and becomes one with the Unity.

Not only the scriptures but practical Hinduism accepts all forms of God worship. However, dualism and non-dualism are two main representative forms of Hindu metaphysics. The worshipper is his best judge as, many a time, even the intellectuals have found it convenient to worship on idols symbolic of their favorite deities because all serious worshippers, after reaching a certain stage, get lost into the ecstasy of the divine love and need no form or symbol as they are supposed to have become one with the Supreme Being.

Devotees who became one with God became God incarnates themselves like Ramakrishna or Chaitanya Mahaprabhu, who lived not very long ago, and hundreds of very well-known saints and seers in all countries and in all ages. These persons were gods in human form, and considered others as divines. For example, to Androcles, the God was in the lion who became his friend and licked his feet; but the great Sanskrit

---

[1] Will Durant, Our Oriental Heritage, p. 549

grammarian Rishi Panini was so much charmed by the God in a lion in the forest, where he was teaching his students, that he couldn't resist being separate from the God in the lion, and he ran to embrace him only to be killed by him.

यं ब्रह्मा वरुणेन्द्ररुद्रमरुतः स्तुन्वन्ति दिव्यैः स्तवै-
र्वेदैः साङ्गपदक्रमोपनिषदैर्गायन्ति यं सामगाः ।
ध्यानावस्थिततद्गतेन मनसा पश्यन्ति यं योगिनो
यस्यान्तं न विदुः सुरासुरगणा देवाय तस्मै नमः ॥

SUPREME SPIRIT AND MATERIAL NATURE PURUSH AND PRAKRITI

SUPREME SPIRIT CONSORTING WITH HIS PARAMOUR THE NATURE.

SUMMARY OF HINDU METAPHYSICS
(SHRIMAD BHAGVADGITA)

In the Hindu worship there is no place for blind worship through one and only one mode of worship. Since the worshipper's objective is to realize or to see Him face to face, he monitors his experience as he progresses in his meditation. As Swami Vivekanand says: "The goal is to manifest this Divine within, by controlling nature, external and internal. Do this either by work, or worship or psychic control, or philosophy - by one or more or all of these - and be free. This is the whole crux of religion. Doctrines or dogmas, or rituals or books, or temples or forms are but secondary details."[1] Therefore, an intellectual blend of science and faith is essential for attainment of moksha. Nevertheless good teachers do impart knowledge and awareness to the worshipper, of the whole tradition of the shastrakars, the seers, the saints and the yogis who, through their own contemplation, meditation, or sadhna found explanations of the Unknown, gave guidelines, and even showed supernatural in them to make the spiritual experience believable.

Most of the principles of Hindu philosophy are summed up in the Bhagvadgita as the sermon of Lord Krishna to Arjuna on the battlefield of Kurukshetra. The Gita, as it is commonly known, is a poem of seven hundred verses spread over 18 chapters in the great Hindu epic of the Mahabharata which narrates the story of the descendants of King Bharata, popularly known as Kauravs and Pandavs, who fought a destructive civil war about five thousand years ago. The epic Mahabharata is a drama of exceptionally transporting literary skill running into over one hundred thousand verses, seven times the Iliad and the Odyssey together. The author of the epic is sage Ved

---

[1] Romain Rolland, Life and Gospel of Vivekananda, p. 271

Vyasa, son of Rishi Parashar and the celebrated compiler of the Vedas, 'who was inspired by Brahma, the Creator' into writing this epic with the purpose of spreading the eternal message that the good prevails over the evil eventually.

Bhagvan Ved Vyasa summarized all essentials of Hindu philosophy into the Gita so that persons of all interests and inclinations could find their way of worship and realization at one place without looking for guidance elsewhere. That is why in the Mahabharta, after narrating the Gita, Rishi Ved Vyasa said:

> Gita sugita kartabya
> kimanya sastra wistrei,
> ya swayam padmanabhysya
> mukhpadmad vinistrita.[2]

meaning: If Gita which has been spoken by Bhagwan Vishnu himself can be fully digested, then there remains no need to go to learn any other scriptures.

Another well-known verse from Vaisnaviya Tantrasara says this:

> sarvopanisado gavo dogdha gopalnandanah,
> partho vatsah sudhir bhokta
> dugdham gitamrtam mahat.

Meaning: The Gita is the essence of all the teachings of the Upanishadas. The analogy in the verse means that the Upanishadas are the cows; krishna, the cowherd, is the milker; Arjuna is the calf; the

---

[2] गीतासुगीताकर्तव्याकिमन्यैः शास्त्रविस्तरैः।
या स्वयं पद्मनाभस्य मुखपद्माद्विनिःसृता ॥

wise man is the drinker; and the nectar-like Gita is the milk.

Aldous Huxley removes the Gita from the lap of the Hindus and gives it to the whole world saying that its usefulness is not just for the Indians; the Gita is for the whole world as in it he finds the most comprehensive summaries of the spiritual thoughts ever to have been made: "The Gita is one of the clearest and most comprehensive summaries of the Perennial Philosophy ever to have been made. Hence its enduring value, not only for Indians, but for all mankind."[4] Wilhelm von Humboldt pronounced it "the most beautiful, perhaps the only true philosophical song existing in any known tongue . . . . perhaps the deepest and loftiest thing the world has to show."[5]

The first harbinger of American religious freedom in Massachusetts, Henry David Thoreau is said to have come across a fresh translation of the Gita by Burnouf but certainly the one by Charles Jones which had just been published those days. Dissatisfied with all other philosophies, he loved the newfound thought which he wanted to carry to the end of the earth. His new religion was the Gita for which he said this:

> "In the morning I bathe my intellect in the stupendous and cosmogonal philosophy of the Bhagvadgita, in comparison with which our modern world and its literature seem puny and trivial."

---

[4] Aldous Huxley, Introduction to the Bhagvadgita by Swami Prabhavananda and Christopher Isherwood (1945)

[5] Will Durant, Our Oriental Heritage, p. 565

Ralph Waldo Emerson was inspired by Thoreau into the Vedantic philosophy of which he became so obsessed and emotional that he founded the "Transcendental Club"[6] and edited The Dial, its quarterly, with the aim of spreading the nature's eternal religion of his Aryan forefathers into the new world so that in the new land they should have their own religion.[7] The famous poem `Brahma' is an example of his Vedantic ecstasy. This is what he says about the Gita:

> "I owed a magnificent day to the Bhagavad-gita. It was as if an empire spoke to us, nothing small or unworthy, but large, serene, consistent, the voice of an old intelligence which in another age and climate had pondered and thus disposed of the same questions which exercise us."

Mohandas K. Gandhi, the well-known apostle of non-violence and human freedom and the father of the Indian nation took all his inspiration from the Gita and found all his questions answered therein. This is what he says on the Gita:

> "When doubts haunt me, when disappointments stare me in the face, and I see not one ray of hope on the horizon, I turn to Bhagvadgita and find a verse to comfort me; and I immediately begin to smile in the midst of overwhelming sorrow. Those who meditate on the Gita will derive fresh joy and new meanings from it every day."

People are disposed to thinking, working and loving. They

---

[6] Romain Rolland, Life and Gospel of Vivekananda, p. 49

[7] Not the abstract secularist idealism, but the common man's zeal, backed by force of arms and love of material gains was the requirement then to spread a religion - the kind that was available to the most early marauders in the new world.

adopt new ways of jnana, karma and bhakti respectively for attainment of liberation from the bondage of the cycle of birth and death. These ways are explained in detail in the Gita in a simple question-answer form in order to remove Arjuna's delusion about the true meaning of life, death, life after death, soul and salvation in this world. To convince him that he has to do his duty, Krishna does not merely argue with him that fighting is his caste duty as a warrior but reveals to him His cosmic personality to show to him that he is just an infinitesimal part of it, and he is merely a pawn moved by the hand of an all-powerful God, which He himself is, and whose will no man or god can resist. He wants him to do the work for the sake of work. The Gita preaches work without hankering after its fruits (nishkam karma) by staying on duty where one is stationed. The Gita does not preach war. Its dictum is to keep moving in the mainstream, with a heart for any fate which is determined only by one's own karmas. Incidentally, the Gita does not teach Ahimsa (non-injury to living beings) as some Ahimsa zealots have thought. Being earlier in time to Buddha, Ahimsa as such was perhaps unknown to the Vedic age; and it does not relate to the main problem arising at the crucial moment when the Gita was spoken. Prof. Franklin Edgerton says, that Gita pays only lip-homage to the doctrine which term appears mentioned therein unimportantly.[8]

"In fact, the Bhagvadgita's immediate aim is to inspire the reluctant Arjuna to do his duty as a Kshatriya and fight the battle of righteousness, destroy the evil without feeling qualms at slaying those who support it."[9]

---

[8] The nowin showdown between Ashwathama and Arjuna in the end of the war can be shown to suggest that non-violence is an alternative.

[9] W. Norman Brown, <u>Mythologies of Ancient World</u>, p. 317

On page 11 of his book, the Bhagvadgita, Dr. Radhakrishnan has given an important quotation of J.W. Hauer, a missionary in India and an official exponent of "the German faith", and a Sanskrit scholar, who gave to the Gita, a central place in the German faith. He declares that the book "gives us not only profound insights that are valid for all time and all religious life, but it contains as well the classical presentation of one of the most significant phases of Indo-Germanic religious history... Here spirit is at work that belongs to our spirit." He states the central message of the Gita in these words: "We are not called to solve the meaning of life but to find out the Deed demanded of us and to work and so, by action, to master the riddle of life.[10]

Through the freedom of thought and action that Hinduism arms the individual in his quest for perfection, Gita suggests four important ways to attain moksha -salvation. These four ways are four yogas: Jnana Yoga, Karma Yoga, Raja Yoga, and Bhakti Yoga. Jnana is the ultimate state, but it has to be reached with the help of other yogas such as Raj yoga, Karma Yoga and Bhakti Yoga, the latter two being more popular. Even each of these yogas are independently capable of getting moksha to the practicant; but as the aspirant proceeds in his yogic experience, he necessarily tends to acquire elements of the other yogas and attains perfection because perfection is the ultimate goal of all the yogas. And theory and practice have the same end result as Lord Krishna answers Arjuna's question in Chapter 5 of the Gita thus:

Arjuna said:

5.1[11] <u>samnyasam</u> karmanam, krsna, punar

---

[10] Dr. Radhakrishnan, <u>The Bhagvadgita</u>, p.11
   (Quoted in Hibbert Journal, April 1940, p. 341)

[11] संन्यासं कर्मणां कृष्ण पुनर्योगं च शंससि ।
   यच्छ्रेय एतयोरेकं तन्मे ब्रूहि सुनिश्चितम् ॥

Summary of Hindu Metaphysics

> yogam ca samsasi
> yac chreya etayor ekam tan me bruhi
> suniscitam.

meaning: O Krishna, you suggest renunciation (sanyas) and then you propose unattached works (nishkam karam). Which one is the better of the two? Tell me this in clear decisive words!

Krishna answers:

5.5[12] yat samkhyaih prapyate sthanam tad
yogair api gamyate;
ekam samkhyam ca yogam ca:
yah pasyati sa pasyati.

meaning: It is true that the men of theory (philosophy) attain a high position, but that the same state is achieved by the men of practice (karam yogis) too, for theory and practice are both one and the same thing: he who sees this correctly does see all things clearly and truly.

Yet like a modern teacher, Krishna, the God incarnate, does not impose this doctrine on his disciple or on his audience, for that matter. He only counsels Arjuna; and after giving all his lecture, in the end, He tells that "It is my opinion; you are at liberty to do whatever you think is right for you." Shloka 63 of Chapter 18 provides this:

> iti te jnanam akhyatam guhyad guhyatram   maya,
> vimrsyai' tad asesena yathe' cchasi tatha   kuru.[13]

---

12   यत्सांख्यैः प्राप्यते स्थानं तद्योगैरपि गम्यते ।
एकं सांख्यं च योगं च यः पश्यति स पश्यति ॥

13   तुमसे कहा अतिगुप्त ज्ञान समस्त यह विस्तार से ।
जिस भाँति जो चाहे वही कर पार्थ ! पूर्ण विचार से ॥

Now this is the greatest example of the freedom in God worship in Hinduism when the Lord `God' Himself does not compel people to have faith in only Him or incite in them fears of doom and damnation as punishment for disbelieving.

We now move to the theory and the practice contained in the yogas.

OUR MINDS ARE VEILED SUPER-MINDS.

THE YOGAS:
(Four Great Paths in the Gita)

I. *Janana Yoga:*

Jnana Yoga is not just intellectual knowledge of a branch or two of learning, nor is it the knowledge of all mundane or spiritual things, but is the knowledge of the All. It is to be part of the All or to be wisdom personified, Brahman Himself. It is intuitive aperception of the Ultimate Reality.[1] It is the knowledge that liberates and is distinct from all intellectual knowledge of the world or the physical and mental things which bind. According to Radhakrishnan, "it is absence of ignorance. So long as ignorance persists, it is not possible to escape from the vicious circle of becoming. We cannot cure desires by fresh desires; we cannot cure action by more action. The eternal cannot be gained by that which is temporal. Whether we are bound by good desires or bad desires, it is still a question of bondage. It makes little difference whether the chains which bind us are made of gold or of iron. To escape from bondage, we must get rid of ignorance.[2] When the ignorance is gone, wisdom (jnana) is attained. Jnana in this context becomes the means and the end or both. When it is the means, it is action or karma as discussed under Karma Yoga next following; but when it is the end, it is the ultimate stage - pure, perfect and absolute (Satchitananda). It is the union with God Himself wherein all works are reduced to ashes; and there remains no desires for work or worship as all desires of the body and the soul are fulfilled. The Lord God Krishna says this in the Gita:

---

[1] Cp. Hegel: "... The highest kind of knowledge must be that possessed by the Absolute, and as the Absolute is the Whole, there is nothing outside Itself to know."

[2] S. Radhakrishnan, Bhagvadgita, p. 52

4.33[3]   sreyan dravyamayad yajnaj jnanayajnah, paramtapa,
sarvam karm'akhilam, Partha, jnane parisamapyate.

Meaning: Acquisition and dispensation of knowledge as a sacrifice (yajna) to attain moksha is greater than any material sacrifice, for all material sacrificial works find their consummation in wisdom.

4.37[4]   yath'aidhamsi samiddho'gnir bhasmsat kurute'rjuna,
jnan'agnih savra-karmani bhasmasat kurute tatha.

Meaning: Just as fire reduces its fuel to ashes, in the same way the fire of wisdom consumes all works, good or evil.

4.38[5]   nahi jnanena sadrsam pavitram iha vidyate;
tat svayam yoga-samsiddhah kalen'atmani vindati.

Meaning: For there is nothing on earth so pure as wisdom; and in course of time, a man himself can find this wisdom within himself. In other words, as a yogi goes ahead in his practice, he gets perfection, the all-knowledgeable state which is the union with the Ultimate Brahman, Krishna

4.41[6]   yoga-samnyasta-karmanam jnana-
samchinna-samsayam

---

[3] श्रेयान्द्रव्यमयाद्यज्ञाज्ज्ञानयज्ञः परंतप ।
सर्वं कर्माखिलं पार्थ ज्ञाने परिसमाप्यते ॥

[4] यथैधांसि समिद्धोऽग्निर्भस्मसात्कुरुतेऽर्जुन ।
ज्ञानाग्निः सर्वकर्माणि भस्मसात्कुरुते तथा ॥

[5] न हि ज्ञानेन सदृशं पवित्रमिह विद्यते ।
तत्स्वयं योगसंसिद्धः कालेनात्मनि विन्दति ॥

[6] योगसंन्यस्तकर्माणं ज्ञानसंछिन्नसंशयम् ।
आत्मवन्तं न कर्माणि निबध्नन्ति धनंजय ॥

atmavantam na karmani nibadhanti,
dhanamjaya.

Meaning: O winner of wealth (Arjuna), works do not bind the person who, integrated in himself, is engaged in unselfish works and whose all doubts have been destroyed through wisdom.

4.42[7] tasmad ajnana-sambhutam hrt-stham
jnan'asina'tmanah
chittv'ainam samsayam yogam
atisth'ottistha, Bharata.

Meaning: Therefore, take up the sword of wisdom, and with it cut all your doubts, which are born of ignorance that is still lurking in your heart: prepare for action now, get up, O Arjuna!

Jnana Yoga, like other three yogas, aims at integration with the Absolute Being. "It invokes both Science and reason in uncertain tones,"[8] and recognizes experience as the source of knowledge. Hindu thought in Jnana Yoga as well as in other yogas, does not accept magic or miracle for attaining liberation. One has to work one's way upward. Eulogizing reason, the devoted complementary of jnana, Swami Vivekananda observes: "It has been said that reason is not strong enough; it does not always help us to get to the Truth; many times it makes mistakes, and therefore, the conclusion is that we must believe in the authority of a church. That was said to me by a Roman Catholic, but I could not see the logic of it. On the other hand, I should say, if reason be so weak, a body of priests would be weaker, and I am not going to accept their verdict, but I will abide by my reason, because

---

[7] तस्मादज्ञानसंभूतं हृत्स्थं ज्ञानासिनात्मनः ।
छित्त्वैनं संशयं योगमातिष्ठोत्तिष्ठ भारत ॥

[8] Romain Rolland, <u>Life and Gospel of Vivekananda</u>, p. 235

with all the weakness there is some chance of my getting at truth through it . . . We should, therefore, follow reason, and also sympathize with those who do not come to any sort of belief, following reason. For it is better that mankind should become atheist by following reason than blindly believe millions of gods on the authority of any body. What we want is progress . . . . No theories ever made man higher . . . . The only power is in realization and that lies in ourselves and comes from thinking. The glory of man is that he is a thinking being . . . . I believe in reason and follow reason, having seen enough of the evils of authority, for I was born in a country where they have gone to the extreme of authority."[9] Again he says: "Do you not see whither science is tending? The Hindu nation proceeds through the study of the mind, through metaphysics and logic. The European nations start from external nature, and now they too are coming to the same result. We find that searching through the mind we at last come to that Oneness, that Universal One, the Internal Soul of everything, the Essence, the Reality of everything . . . . Through material science we come to the same Oneness...."[10]

Knowledge is power and infinite knowledge is infinite power - Omnipotence (sarvashakti) which is God Almighty. The starting point and methods of Jnana Yoga are much like those of the modern scientific spirit of the West. Science and reason are its two great tools, and personal effort employing logic and reason has been the only basis for attaining jnana in Hinduism, as against any magic, miracle or mercy. This yoga encourages the practicant to be knowledgeable in arts, sciences, metaphysics and all other mysterious and esoteric things employing reason in their study and accept nothing blindly from any one. Hinduism does not accept religion on faith though faith is an important

---

[9] Practical Vedanta III, p. 335-36

[10] Complete Works of Swami Vivekananda, Vol. I, p. 140

requisite of the character of the devotee. Here seeing is believing. That is why Hindu seers and saints were not satisfied without seeing Him or their respective deities face to face. Even Arjuna was reluctant to believe and accept what his mentor and bosom friend Lord Krishna said about his far-flung powers without seeing his Universal Form.

It is amusing to know of the usual complaint of some missionaries in India and abroad, and in the U.S. too that Hindus do not care for the literature presented to them for believing the things written in them. The Hindus do respect all other religions with the same respect as they show to their own religion knowing that their saints like Ramakrishsna Paramhansa, and reformers like Raja Ram Mohan Roy have been the known worshipper of Christianity. But they do not easily accept a faith other than their own, even the one from variety of them in Hindu ism. Religion to them is not a dogma; it is a sort of working relationship and used for help and support for a good life in this world and a better state in the life to come unless he could do something in this very life so he does not have to return to this world again. A few important topics used in the Hindu thought are explained next.

OUR DEEDS (KARMAS) DERMINE OUR DESTINIES.

LORD GOD KRISHNA IN THE GITA

Krishna, the Lord God, is expressed in the Gita from both dualist and non-dualist angle so that a special non-dualism is developed. He is the totality of all forms and also takes a form when He incarnates himself in a human body to help rehabilitate dharma and punish the wrongdoers. In non-dualist abstract thinking, He is a formless totality, and the source of the eternal world of changeless and the phenomenal world. In the Gita He is both, but is also beyond the both. This is Vishistadvaitvad of the eleventh century philosopher Ramanujacharya which may be summarized as under:

This universe can be divided in two parts, matter and spirit translated as maya and jiva in Hinduism. Matter is the cause of this changing world of forms and senses in living beings including mind and soul. This is the world of change. Spirit is the totality of souls in this universe which have their independent existence. They attach themselves to the psychosomatic organisms of their choice, indwell them for as long as it takes for liberation from matter, and on liberation merge into the ambiance that is conditioned neither by Time or Space. This is the world of changeless. These two segments of matter and spirit constitute the 'body' of the Lord "The Lord God is the soul of this body just as the 'embodied' self is the soul of each human individual." God is the center of this active universe of matter and the totality of spirits in the same way as the embodied self is the center of the changing organism of matter and spirit in a living body. His description in Svetasvatara Upanishad (5.1) is close to the following verse:

> "In the imperishable, infinite city of Brahman
> Two things there are -
> Wisdom and unwisdom, hidden, established
> There;
> Perishable is unwisdom, but wisdom is
> Immortal;
> Who over wisdom and unwisdom rules,
> He is another."[1]

Krishna is an incarnation of God in the Gita. In accordance with his claim in the Gita that "whenever there is loss of dharma and the devilish forces are on the increase in this world, then I manifest myself ." He has been manifesting himself into forms of living beings, especially in human form recognizable to humans. He came as a friend, a teacher, a guide, and showed to his dear friend Arjuna that he has to establish order; and if you as an important hero of this human drama will not act the right way, he himself will. Being a good democrat he wants the parties to settle their problems themselves, preferably by peaceful means, or by war without any other choice. And he succeeded in establishing the peace, order, and the law of dharma.

The poet of the Gita presents Krishna, as the most supreme, and higher than the totality of the material objects and the totality of the spiritual monads. He is shown to be beyond anything and everything, yet controls and commands the All. The poet has a purpose in depicting God as the Most High when Krishna reveals Himself to Arjuna in the `virat form' which is what Arjuna, perhaps not a philosopher, was capable of understanding. Thus the poet tries to teach the humans that they, being infinitesimal part of the Totality, have no choice but to keep moving in His mighty Wheel of Karma, as none can will against His Will which wills any way regardless of their own little

---

[1] R. C. Zaehner, The Bhagvadgita, p. 9

wills acting in their own "little world" because the result in the context of the universal law of Karma is already ordained by Him. Krishna, therefore, urges Arjuna to get up, do the fighting, and win glory as all his enemies are already slain ; and he should only act as his appointed agent.

TRANSMIGRATION OF SOUL

"Like corn decays the mortal," said the Katha Upanishad, "like corn is he born again." It is one of the fundamental tenets of Hinduism that the soul, upon the death of one body, moves to another body or form carrying with it all the impressions or deeds that it has accumulated in its previous body. It is a simple cause and effect process between the matter and the spirit, the soul. At the end of a life, the effect can condition the soul to find a niche in conformance with the impressions it has received in the previous life. All living beings are subject to this process of transmigration since they began life. Once they are born, they return again and again after the death of their bodies until their entrapped souls or spirits are released from the cycle of birth and death. The release is sooner or later depending upon the deeds (karmas) done.

As each one of us has differing material properties, so do we carry differing psychological abilities. This difference in us is more explained through the theory of reincarnation than by any other reason. Mere heredity or environment or chemistry of the brain wouldn't explain why two children, born of the same parents, living in the same house, and raised up in the same situations, grow up poles apart: one is a noble scholar, but the other turns out to be a devilish person spending his life in jail. And what is the explanation for the glory of a person born rich and the misery of another born poor respectively in the rich and the poor families except primarily as a result of their deeds in their previous lives? We aare born into this world with our experiences of previous lives; and the fortune or misfortune of this existence is the result of our acts in a former existence, always becoming better or worse till at last perfection is reached. There is no chance happening in the working of Nature because all objects of nature have their automatic and orderly movements. The sun, the moon, the planets, the rains, the seasons, the vegetation, the insects, the animals, the humans, and the gods - all incarnations of the Supreme Spirit, appear and disappear, in endless cycles working by virtue of their inherent properties (gunas) and in accordance with their previously acquired deeds (karmas).

Shrimad Bhagvadgita dwells on the phenomenon of transmigration in Chapter 15: The Eternal Fig-tree. Beside others, shloka 15.8 says: "When the sovereign self takes on a body and when he rises up therefrom, he takes them with him and moves on as the wind wafts scents away from their power home." [1]

carry over tendencies mastered in our previous lives. This transference is natural and effortless like the movements of the fingers of a typist on to a computer. Just as these practitioners acquire tendencies and conditioning so do the souls in their previous lives; and travelling from life to life, they get better or worse till their release on perfection. Lord God Krishna has been incarnating Himself: He says this to Arjuna in answer to a question in the Gita:

4.5[2]   bahuni me vyatitani janamani
         tava c'arjuna:
         any aham veda sarvani, na tvam   vettha,
paramtapa.

Meaning: Many a birth have I gone through and many a birth have you: I know them all, but you do not, O, Arjuna!

Buddha is said to have had countless previous lives. Jesus Christ confirms this when he said: "Before Abraham was, I

---

1   बहूनि मे व्यतीतानि जन्मानि तव चार्जुन ।
    तान्यहं वेद सर्वाणि न त्वं वेत्थ परंतप ॥

2   न जायते म्रियते वा कदाचिन्नायं भूत्वा भविता वा न भूयः ।
    अजो नित्यः शाश्वतोऽयं पुराणो न हन्यते हन्यमाने शरीरे ॥

am."³ Time and again, we have come across news of the children telling of the memories of their previous lives; and there are well-known stories wherein they identified previous relations.

The individual self is that miniature part of purusha, the universal spirit, which got trapped into matter through cosmic process and has been awaiting release from the bondage. To Hegel, it is self-contained existence: "It is one immutably homogeneous Infinite-pure Identity - which, in its second phase, separates itself from itself and makes this second aspect its own polar opposite, namely as existence for and in Self as contrasted with the Universal."⁴ The soul separates itself from its Father, the Supreme Soul, through ignorance and entrapment by nature (maya).

According to Dr. Radhakrishnan, "The soul's substantial existence springs from the Divine intellect and its expression in life is affected by virtue of its vision of the Divine who is its father and its ever-present companion. Its distinctiveness is determined by the divine pattern and the context of the senses and the mind which it draws to itself. The Universal is embodied in a limited context of mental vital-physical sheath . . . . The jivas are movements in the being of God, individualized. When the ego is lost in a false identification with the not-self and its forms, it is bound; but when through the development of proper understanding, it realizes the true nature of the self and the non-self and allows the apparatus produced by the not-self to be illumined completely by the self, then it is freed.⁵ He cannot be happy unless and untill the bond of attachment is broken and he is liberated.⁶

---

[3] John, viii, p.58

[4] Bertrand Russell, A History of Western Philosophy, p.737

[5] S. Radhakrishnanan, Bhagvadgita, p.45

[6] सो मायाबस भयउ गोसाईं ※ बँध्यो कीर मरकट की नाईं,
तब ते जीव भयउ संसारी ※ छूट न ग्रन्थि न होइ सुखारी

After Arjuna refuses to fight the civil war at Kurukshetra, the first topic that Krishna discusses in his dialogue with him is the nature of the embodied self. He establishes the immortality of the embodied self in the following verses of the Gita since Arjuna was basically scared of the death of all his kinsmen and of himself in the war that was to start imminently:

2.20[7] na jayate mriyate va kadacin
n'ayam bhutva bhavite va na bhuyah:
ajo nityah sasvato'yam purano,
na hanyate hanyamane sarire.

Meaning: The soul is never born nor dies; or it never came to be nor will it ever come to be again. It is unborn, eternal, everlasting and primeval. It is not slain when the body is slain.[1] It is beyond time and space. Uninvolved with the body, it is participating in or is identical with the Brahman. Because of our limited consciousness, the self in us appears separate from the whole. In fact, it is a part of the whole.

2.22[8] vasamsi jirnani yatha vihayes
navani grahanati naro'parani,
tatha sarirani vihaya jirnany
anyani samyati navani dehi.

Meaning: As a person discards his old clothes and puts on the new

---

[7] न जायते म्रियते वा कदाचिन्नायं भूत्वा भविता वा न भूयः ।
अजो नित्यः शाश्वतोऽयं पुराणो न हन्यते हन्यमाने शरीरे ॥

[8] वासांसि जीर्णानि यथा विहाय नवानि गृह्णाति नरोऽपराणि ।
तथा शरीराणि विहाय जीर्णान्यन्यानि संयाति नवानि देही ॥

ones, so does the embodied self enters the new body after leaving the old ones.

2.23[9] n'ainam chindanti sastrani n'ainam dahati pavakah
na c'ainam kladayanty apo, na sosayati marutah.

Meaning: Weapons do not cut it nor does the fire burn it. Water does not wet it nor does the wind dry it.

2.28[10] avyakt'adini bhutani vyakta madhyani, Bharata,
avyakta-nidhanany eva: tatra ka paridevana

Meaning: All contingent beings are unmanifest in the beginning; they are manifest in the middle when born and living in this world. They become unmanifest again on dying. Then why worry, O, Arjuna?

It is, therefore, clear in the Gita, as in all other Hindu scriptures, that the embodied self is immortal as a timeless monad, a minute part of the Universal Spirit or God. Souls are part of Him like the sparks from a burning firewood. As the sparks have the burning firewood nearby so do the souls have their Supreme Soul around.[11] It is never born with the body nor dies with the body. It is original, eternal,

---

[9] नैनं छिन्दन्ति शस्त्राणि नैनं दहति पावकः ।
न चैनं क्लेदयन्त्यापो न शोषयति मारुतः ॥
Cp. Emerson in Brahma:
If the red slayer thinks he slays
or if the slain thinks he is slain
they know not well the subtle ways
I keep, and pass, and turn again.
अव्यक्तादीनि भूतानि व्यक्तमध्यानि भारत ।
[10] अव्यक्तनिधनान्येव तत्र का परिदेवना ॥

[11] Cp. Susu: "All creatures have existed eternally in the Divine essence as in their examplar. So far as they conform to the Divine idea, all beings were before their cration, one with the essence of God." Quoted from Radhakrishnan, Bhagvadgita, p.103

and everlasting. But as it is linked through entrapment with an individual psychosomatic organism which is maya or nature, it appears to be born and dead with the body. It is merely a witness at the act played by the body with its mind, soul and senses; but its vision is limited to the size and stature of the body and, of course, its ignorance. The embodied self is the part of eternal psychical principle different from the eternal physical principle, such as, body, senses, mind and intellect, the material nature - the maya - in which the embodied self lies imprisoned. Its release or salvation lies in complete detachment of the embodied self from the material nature (maya) which is possible through complete knowledge, detached works, the intense concentration or meditation into the Supreme Self, or prayers, or through all of these. All these methods aim at liberating the embodied self which, once liberated, pervades into the Infinite and becomes one with Him after losing its individual existence. It is then Brahman or God Himself.

ALL ARE DIVINE BEINGS IN MORE OR LESS DEGREES.

MATERIAL NATURE

"The real exterior universe is an unknown x. The universe that we know is x + (or -) the mind, in its function of perceptive faculty, which gives it the imprint of its own conditions. The mind can only know itself through the medium of the mind which is an unknown y + (or -) the condition of the mind... Centuries before Kant Vedantic philosophy had already predicted and even surpassed it."[1] According to Sankhya system of Rishi Kapila, Nature (Prakriti) is the universal physical principle which is animated, vitalized and stimulated into productive process with the help of universal psychical principle known as Supreme Spirit (Purusha). The proximity of Purusha to Prakriti, similar to male and female, like loadstone to iron, causes the latter to produce the animate and inanimate objects of this univerase in accordance with matter's three properties (gunas) known as sattva (purity), rajas (passion) and tamas (darkness). It is the movement of three gunas and their combination in different proportions that creates the visible universe."[2]

To put it differently, the interaction of matter and spirit creates disequilibrium out of which comes the cosmos with its pain and suffering. Equilibrium results or peace returns from withdrawing spirit from its involvement with matter. This interaction does not suggest that matter is in any way evil. It is a statement of the fact of the existence of the process in the evolution.

There is the vast evolving and dissolving froth of matter and mind which is Nature (prakriti) along side the quiet eternity of Supreme Spirit (Purusha). Maya (Nature) as explained by Sant Tulsidas is all and

---

[1] Romain Rolland, Life and Gospel of Vivekananda, p. 240

[2] Ishvarkrishna, Sankhya Karika, I: 33-69, pp.308-14

everything. It extends upto and beyond the objects of senses and mind, and includes I, my, you, and your - everything that has captured all the living beings. It is wisdom and unwisdom both.[3]

"Maya cannot be defined as non-existence any more than it can be defined as existence: It is an intermediate form between the equally absolute Being and non-Being. . . . It is not existence, for, says the Hindu Vedantist, its is the sport of the Absolute. It is not non-Existence, because this sport exists and we cannot deny it."[4] The mother Nature is a part of Him - the inherent part of Him, the Unmanifest and Eternal. Because He is Swayambhu, He at his will which has an eternal moral order, manifests Himself into this world of material Nature and then, following a pattern, unmanifests Himself, rather dissolves this manifest Nature into the same Supreme Source from which it was born. Bhagvadgita describes it thus:

8.18[5] avyaktad vyaktayah sarvah prabhavanty
ahar-agame;
ratry-agme praliyante
tatr'aiv'vyakta-samjnake.

Meaning: At the day's dawning all things spring forth from the Unmanifest; and then at nightfall they dissolve in that same thing called Unmanifest.

8.19[6] bhuta-gramah sa ev'ayam bhutva bhutva

---

[3] Sant Tulsidas in the Ramayana (Aranyakand):

[4] Romain Rolland, Life and Gospel of Vivekananda, p. 182

[5] अव्यक्ताद्व्यक्तय: सर्वा: प्रभवन्त्यहरागमे ।
रात्र्यागमे प्रलीयन्ते तत्रैवाव्यक्तसंज्ञके ॥

[6] भूतग्राम: स एवायं भूत्वा भूत्वा प्रलीयते ।
रात्र्यागमेऽवश: पार्थ प्रभवत्यहरागमे ॥

praliyate
ratry-agame'vasah, Partha,
praghavaty ahar-agme

Meaning: This multitudes of beings of matter and spirit keep coming ever anew, O Arjuna, and helplessly dissolve away or die; and at dawn of the day, they wake up or are reborn again.

9.7[7] Saiva-bhutani, Kauntaya, prakrtim yanti mamikam
kalpa-ksaye, punas tani kalp'adau
visrjamy aham.

Meaning: When a world-aeon ends, all contingent beings return into material Nature; and then when another aeon starts, they are manifested forth.

9.8[8] prakrtim svam ayastabhya visrjami punah punah
bhuta-gramam imam krtsnam avasam
prakrter vasat.

Meaning: Seized by my own material Nature, I again and again produce this whole host of beings which is powerless in itself but receives power from Me.

Dr. Radhakrishnan's explanation of this phenomenon is like this: "The unmanifested nature when lit up by the Unmanifested Self

---

[7] सर्वभूतानि कौन्तेय प्रकृतिं यान्ति मामिकाम् ।
कल्पक्षये पुनस्तानि कल्पादौ विसृजाम्यहम् ॥

[8] प्रकृतिं स्वामवष्टभ्य विसृजामि पुनः पुनः ।
भूतग्राममिमं कृत्स्नमवशं प्रकृतेर्वशात् ॥

produces the objective universe with its different planes. The order and nature of development are determined by the seeds contained in nature. Only the Divine Self must take hold of it."[9]

The whole cosmic process is a cycle, and it comes from nowhere except ITSELF. This is evolution which means that the nature of things is reproduced and "that the effect is nothing but the cause in another form, that all the potentialities of the effect were present in the cause, that the whole of creation is but an evolution and not a creation."[10] All are part of this process. It is with the stars, the sun, the moon, the mountains or the mighty seas, and of course with all living beings. Each must die and be reborn again anew like each of us do sleep at night and must wake up at dawn. All are bound into this cycle from the tiniest creature to the Creator Brahma who too, after completing his life of one `hundred' years does die along with his creation and is reborn again along with his creation, according to their karmas, of course. And there are countless Brahmas who appear and disappear like bubbles in the ocean.

In this way all things of material nature - beings and non-beings keep moving in a cycle. The whole process of the births and deaths - comings and goings of all material things, of all seasons, and of all celestial beings is an endless game, the `leela which He plays eternally in a great grand cycle that has no beginning and no end. And all these world and beings of material nature right up to the Brahma's realms dissolve and are reborn again and again.[11] Only he who has `reached' Him is never born again:

---

[9] S. Radhakrishnan, Bhagvadgita, p.241

[10] Romain Rolland, Life and Gospel of Vivekananda, p.248

8.16[12] a brahma-bhuvanal lokah punar-avartino,
'rjuna,
mam upetya tu, Kaunteya, punar-janma
na vidyate.

meaning: The worlds right up to the Brahma's realm, O Arjuna, are subject to the cycle of birth and death; but he who reaches Me is not born again.

The cosmos (the totality of matter and spirit) is nothing but the All-Pervading Reality. What is known to us as matter is, in fact, Energy. This distinction continues so long as we are living beings, conscious of duality or unless we have attained the all-knowlegdeable state of mind. Aurobindo Ghose says that "matter is the substance of one conscious-being phenomenally divided within itself by the action of a Universal Mind." [13] In trying to understand it in a simpler way, we assume that the matter is divided infinitesimally to the minutest part of an atom. What remains lastly is an intangible matter, an almost spiritual support of matter which can be called ether. At this stage, the intangibility of the form is so subtle that it may not be wrong to call it spirit. "...Drawing away from durability of form we draw toward eternity of essence..."[14]

---

11. Cp. Shelley: Worlds on worlds are rolling over
   from creation to decay,
   like the bubbles on a river
   sparkling, bursting, borne away.

12. आब्रह्मभुवनाल्लोकाः पुनरावर्तिनोऽर्जुन ।
मामुपेत्य तु कौन्तेय पुनर्जन्म न विद्यते ॥

13. Aurobindo Ghose, The Life Divine, p. 217

14. Ibid. p.217

त्यक्त्वा कर्मफलासङ्गं नित्यतृप्तो निराश्रयः।
कर्मण्यभिप्रवृत्तोऽपि नैव किंचित्करोति सः॥
न हि देहभृता शक्यं त्यक्तुं कर्माण्यशेषतः।
यस्तु कर्मफलत्यागी स त्यागीत्यभिधीयते॥

II. KARMA YOGA

Karma is work. We all work, bound as we are, into three attributes of Nature, the gunas: sattava, rajas and tamas. All beings are the products of their nature and they act in accordance with the properties inherent in them. Humans, animals, even the gods, have to act per force of their nature. If they don't, the entire cosmos will disintegrate. Of all the living beings humans have the choice to do or not to do any work at all. Animals and lower beings without the thinking faculty have no choice to act, because they are programmed to do limited sensuous work. It is humans only on the highest step of the evolutionary ladder who act and act in accordance with the perfection attained in their previous lives. Lord Krishna says this in the Gila:

3.5[1]   na hi kascit ksanam api jatu tisthay
akarma-krt,
karyate hy avasah karma sarvah
prakrti-jair gunaih.

Meaning: Man cannot stay without work for a moment because every man has to work involuntarily per force of the constituents of Nature.

3.22[2]   na me, Parth', asti kartavyam trisu
lokesu kimcana
n'anavaptam avaptavyam, varta eva ca
karmani.

Meaning: In the three worlds there is nothing that I need to do, nor

---

[1] न हि कश्चित्क्षणमपि जातु तिष्ठत्यकर्मकृत् ।
कायेंते ह्यवशः कर्म सर्वः प्रकृतिजैर्गुणैः ॥
[2] न मे पार्थास्ति कर्तव्यं त्रिषु लोकेषु किंचन ।
नानवाप्तमवाप्तव्यं वर्त एव च कर्मणि ॥

there is anything attainable that I cannot attain, yet I keep working.

3.24[3] utsideyur ime loka na kuryam karma ced aham,
samkarasya ca karta syam, upahanyam imah prajah.

Meaning: If I were not to engage myself in my work, these worlds of mine would perish, and I would be the perpetrator of confusion, destroying all these my creatures.

But the works, good or bad, bind. We will continue to be bound forever if we do not get out of them. "So long as we lead embodied lives, we cannot escape from action. Without work life cannot be sustained. Anandgiri the thirteenth century commentator on Samkara's philosophy points out that he who knows the self is not moved by the gunas, but he who has not controlled the body and the senses is driven to action by the gunas."[4]

Karma Yoga is the doctrine of detached works. Since man bound by gunas has to act, if only for the sake of maintaining life, it is advisable that his actions do not bind him with his material world because all objects of senses condition and control human mind and soul so that human liberation becomes impossible. The only way out is to work in a way that has the effect of not working materialistically. To put it differently, he is advised to work unselfishly rather desirelessly. Work for the sake of work, not for the sake of its profit, should be the aim. This is the substance of the doctrine of Karma Yoga:

---

[3] उत्सीदेयुरिमे लोका न कुर्यां कर्म चेदहम् ।
संकरस्य च कर्ता स्यामुपहन्यामिमाः प्रजाः ॥

[4] S. Radhakrishnan, <u>Bhagvadgita</u>, p. 133

2.47[5] karmany ev'adhikaras te ma phalesu
kdacana:
ma karma-phala-hetur bhur, ma te
sango'stu akarmani.

Meaning: Work alone should be your proper business not the fruit thereof. Your purpose in doing the work should not be the fruit or expectation of it. (But as the result does come naturally) And you don't have to lapse into worklessness (akarmanyata).

2.48[6] yoga-sthah kuru karmani sangam tyaktva
dhanamjya,
siddhy-asiddhyoh samo bhutva samatvam
yoga ucyate.

Meaning: O Arjuna, after giving up attachment to things material and by being same and indifferent in victory and defeat and thus integrated, do all your works. This state of sameness and indifference is called yoga.

3.19[7] tasmad asaktah satatam karyam karma
samacara;
asakto hy acaran karma param apnoti
purusah.

Meaning: Therefore, being detached, perform your duties unceasingly,

---

5 कर्मण्येवाधिकारस्ते मा फलेषु कदाचन ।
    मा कर्मफलहेतुर्भूर्मा ते सङ्गोऽस्त्वकर्मणि ॥

6 योगस्थः कुरु कर्माणि सङ्गं त्यक्त्वा धनञ्जय ।
    सिद्ध्यसिद्ध्योः समो भूत्वा समत्वं योग उच्यते ॥

7 तस्मादसक्तः सततं कार्यं कर्म समाचर ।
    असक्तो ह्याचरन्कर्म परमाप्नोति पूरुषः ॥

because the unattached doer is bound to attain the highest merit and is united with the Supreme Being.

It is not easy to be a karma-yogi as it is not easy to be a jnana-yogi. All yogas are practices, constant sadhnas in which the sadhaks (practicant) has to be engaged with full devotion and regularity. When he is engaged thus, he becomes a different man. His qualities are brought out distinctly in the second chapter of the Gita. One of these wonderful verses reads thus:

2.69[8]   ya nisha sarva-bhutanam tassyam jagarti samyami,
yasyam jagrati bhutani sa nisa pasyato muneh.

Meaning: In what is night for all other persons, therein is awake the man of self-restraint (the karma yogi). When all others are awake and working, that is the night for the karma-yogi. This shloka tries to explain that the karamyogi is different from the common man because his approach to this world is uncommon so that his daily activities are not divided into watertight compartments as day and night both are the same for him. Similarly, his worldly needs and pleasures are different from those of the common man.

In almost all respects, a karma-yogi acts different from the common man. If the worldly man likes to accumulate worldly gains, the karma-yogi is not happy with such gains though he should like to have the bare minimum for his needs. When the commoners find joy in overeating sumptuous foods, the yogi would like to eat with restraint lest the overeating should cause difficulty with his system. If the ordinary man is concerned with his health, the yogi is not overly worried about it as he accepts all bodily and mental pains stoically, and leaves

---

[8] या निशा सर्वभूतानां तस्यां जागर्ति संयमी ।
यस्यां जाग्रति भूतानि सा निशा पश्यतो मुनेः ॥

them on God. "Though the actions of the worldly man and the karmayogi look alike, the karma-yogi's distinction is that he has given up attachment to the fruit of his action, and finds joy in the action itself. The yogi, like the worldly man, eats, drinks, sleeps. But his bhavana, his attitude to these actions, is different."[9]

Swami Vivekananda wants his countrymen to work, work and work, because work alone can bring salvation. To get to spiritualism you have to traverse through materialism and none can avoid it. He, therefore, urges men to get into work and be involved in it selflessly; and that will give them the culture of work for the sake of work. He says: ". . . This world's wheel within wheel is a terrible mechanism; if we put our hands in it, as soon as we are caught, we are gone . . . . We are all being dragged along by this mighty complex world-machine. There are only two ways out of it. One is to give up all concern with the machine, to let it go and stand aside . . . That is very easy to say, but it is almost impossible to do. I do not know whether in twenty millions of men one can do that . . . . If we give up our attachment to this little universe of the senses, we shall be free immediately. The only way to come out of bondage is to go beyond the limitation of law, to give up the clinging to the universe . . . . The other way is not negative but positive . . . . It is to plunge into the world and learn the secret of work . . . . and that is the way of Karma Yoga."[10]

Most of us work for money, material gains or satisfaction of desires, ambitions or passions, in one way or another. The more the profit, the deeper are we absorbed into the working. See the plight of a busy man of business or profession. His material advancement is good for his family or his country, but in his incessant gainful activity, he has

---

[9]   Acharya Vinoba Bhave, Talks on the Gita, p. 33

[10] Romain Rolland, Life and Gospel of Vivekananda, p. 193

lost his soul, so that by involving himself more and more into the maya and its attributes of kam, krodh, lobh and moha (lust, anger, greed and attachment, respectively), he finds it impossible to get out of its shackles. His work, good or bad, has enslaved his embodied self. Through the practice of karma yoga, he can do all his work equally well, even better, without losing himself into worrying about its results which are bound to come any way. In this yoga, he conditions his mind and soul so that he engages in work for the sake of work staying same or indifferent in good or bad, right or wrong, profit or loss, victory or defeat - the state which the Lord God Krishna has repeatedly described in the Gita. Here below is a little rendering of the same thought by the great American poet-philosopher Emerson whose love for the Hindu thought is very well-known:

> "Far or forgot to me is near,
> Shadow and sunlight are the same,
> The vanquished gods to me appear,
> And one to me are shame or fame."

To be able to get to the state of indifference and sameness, the karma yogi has to control kama (desire). Desire to enjoy materialistic things comes by thinking about them or by coming close to them. All habits: smoking, drinking, gambling, money-making, for instance, are caused by coming into contact with those persons who do such things or are involved in them. unfulfillment of desire gives rise to anger. From anger comes confusion, loss of memory and right thinking. Once a person loses his sense of right and wrong, he perishes. The Gita says this in Chapter 2:

2.62[11] . dhyayato visayan pumsah sangas
tesu'pajayate,
sangat samjayate kamah, kamat krodho'bhijayate

---

[11] ध्यायतो विषयान्पुंसः सङ्गस्तेषूपजायते । सङ्गात्संजायते कामः कामात्क्रोधोऽभिजायते ॥

II. Karma Yoga

Meaning: From thinking of the objects of senses comes the desire to enjoy them. Closeness gives rise to lust and from lust is anger born.

2.63[12] karodhat bhavati sammohah, sammohat smrti-vibhramah,
smrti-bhramsad buddhi-naso, buddhi-nasat pranasyati.

Meaning: From anger comes confusion or bewilderment of the mind. From bewilderment of the mind comes loss of memory or right thinking. Once right thinking is destroyed, the man perishes.

Desire for reward is as undesirable as desire for avoidance of the punishment for the wrong done. "If you want the reward, you must also have the punishment. The only way to get out of the punishment is to give up the reward. The only way of getting out of misery is by giving up the idea of happiness, because these two are linked together. The only way to get beyond death is to give up the idea of life; and life and death are the same things looked at from different points."[13] Death and life are the same things as the night and the day. When sleeping at night, we are happy, confident and hopeful that we will awake into the next day brighter and better; death also carries the same hope of a new brighter and better life. So, for the reward of a better life, let us accept the death as cheerfully as we accept the night for the promise of the better day. Desire and work are connected to each other. Normally, there is no work without desire for the fruit of it. So all actions are bound by a desire for gain, but if they are done without expecting reward or fruit thereof, their hold on the soul releases, and

---

[12] क्रोधाद्भवति संमोहः संमोहात्स्मृतिविभ्रमः । स्मृतिभ्रंशाद्बुद्धिनाशो बुद्धिनाशात्प्रणश्यति ॥

[13] Romain Rolland, Life and Gospel of Vivekananda, p. 197

the devotee breathes freedom. A more acceptable way of giving up the fruit of work is to cast all the works on Him and to have no hope or thought of the outcome of the work:

3.30[14]   mayi sarvani karmani samnyasy
adhyatma-cetsa,
nirasir nirmamo bhutva yudhyasva
vigata-jvarah.

Meaning: Therefore, O Arjuna, resigning all your works to Me, and integrated in the self and free from desire and delusion, get into the fighting.

A karma yogi does his work unselfishly or with no desire for reward. The material reward is not important because through work it comes naturally; but the more important thing is to keep the soul from being defiled if the work is done from selfish motive. Therefore, it is advised that the work should be considered a moral duty (kartabya) to be done on Krishna because by doing it on Krishna or `with heart for any fate', he offsets any sin or negative effect of works on the soul which is inherent in all works. The essence being, that desire for reward is the wise man's foe and fire insatiable that overcasts his wisdom. Desirelessness is the secret of yoga sadhna that is advised in the Gita :

3.37[15]   kama esa krodha esa rajo-guna-
samudbhavah,
mah'asano maha-papma: viddhy enam
iha vairinam.

---

[14] मयि सर्वाणि कर्माणि संन्यस्याध्यात्मचेतसा ।
निराशीर्निर्ममो भूत्वा युध्यस्व विगतज्वरः ॥

[15] काम एष क्रोध एष रजोगुणसमुद्भवः ।
महाशनो महापाप्मा विद्ध्येनमिह वैरिणम् ॥

Meaning: Born out of the constituent of rajas (passion), the desire and the anger are wicked and all-devouring like fire. You should know them as your enemies.

3.40[16] . indriyani mano buddhir asy'adhisthanam ucyate;
etair vimohayaty esa, jnanam avrtya dehinam

Meaning: Senses, mind and soul are the spots where the desire lurks and this desire fools the embodied self by destroying wisdom.

3.41[17] tasmat tvam indriyany adau niyamya, Bharat'arsabha,
papmanam prajahi hy enam jnana-vijnana-nasanam.

Meaning: Therefore, O Arjuna, restrain your senses first, and then kill this wicked thing which is the destroyer of jnana and vijnana.

      The basic thing for engaging in Karma Yoga or any other yoga is to restrain the desire through the discriminating intellect which alone is the way for any worthwhile attempt for liberation. In other words, the yoga of renunciation has to be practiced by doing works with no desire for reward or any expectation of it. This counsel seems rather incomprehensible to a common man who is advised to make a living by doing work without expecting its compensation or an expectation of it. The working man is not really advised to throw away the fruits of his labor. What Gita prescribes is the renunciation of the fruits, or the

---

[16] इन्द्रियाणि मनो बुद्धिरस्याधिष्ठानमुच्यते । एतैर्विमोहयत्येष ज्ञानमावृत्य देहिनम् ॥

[17] तस्मात्त्वमिन्द्रियाएयादौ नियम्य भरतर्षभ । पाप्मानं प्रजहि ह्येनं ज्ञानविज्ञाननाशनम् ॥

attachment to them or hankering after the material gains, not the just and fair compensation or reward for honest work which does come when the work is done right. The whole idea is why fuming for it when it has to come ultimately because it has been done. It will not come if it is not done or done wrongfully. The poet of the Gita is conscious of the fact that if the compensation is wrongfully denied to the worker, he will cease to have the motivation for good work with the result that he will not only be prevented from doing good to himself and to the society , but also he will have difficulty preserving his physical existence which is contrary to dharma as according to "sreeram adyam khalu dharam sadhnam", a healthy body is the means to achieve salvation. The confusion is removed by suggesting the alternative that all work should be devoted to God or done for His purpose, or they are done with the thought of doing nothing while doing everything because "...In this state you will have passed beyond good and evil, for a man who has reached a state where there is no sense of "I", whose soul is undefiled - were he to slaughter all these worlds - slays nothing. He is not bound."[18]

The yogi may have to pass through numerous lives on way to the liberation of the soul since it got trapped into the psychosomatic organism. It can move up and down the ladder of progress; but with yogic sadhanas and nishkam karmas the liberation is assured. This is the normal way. However, the Hindu mind has miraculously devised a mechanism known as Raja Yoga which breaks the cause and effect process and accelerates the liberation: "The teacher of the Gita recognizes a realm of reality where karma does not operate, and if we establish our relations with it, we are free in our deepest being. The chain of karma can be broken here and now within the flux of the empirical world.[19]

---

[18] R. C. Zaehner, The Bhagvadgita, p. 19

[19] S. Radhakrishnan, Bhagvadgita, p.71

III. RAJA YOGA

Psycho-physical practices for mind cure have been part of Hindu medical science in the ancient times and no wonder Dr. Freud and other modern psychologists are just the beginners in the field discovering the age-old science. "Indian yoga is experimental psychology. Patanjali's Yoga-Sutra, the Upanishads - these and the Saiva Siddhanta treatises - furnish pioneering examples of experimental psychology."[1] "In Indian psychology they proceed from the basis of the supremacy of mind over matter and postulate Atman as the ultimate Reality of the universe"[2] unification with which is the basic purpose of this yoga.

Romain Rolland calls this yoga as the experimental psycho-physiological method for the direct attainment of Reality which is Brahman. Many serious seekers have successfully tried direct realization of the Supreme through the mind control without waiting for indefinite births to take place. This great methodology was developed by the great classical theorist Rishi Patanjali who sought to attain ultimate knowledge through the control and absolute mastery of the mind thus cutting down the endless path of the soul for perfection through future births. The whole thrust is on the concentration and control of mind after shutting it out of all worldly objects to reach the Ultimate Reality. "Normally we waste our energies. Not only are they squandered in all directions by the tornado of exterior impressions; but even when we manage to shut doors and windows, we find chaos within ourselves, a multitude like the one that greeted Julius Caesar in

---

[1] Dr. C. P. Ramaswamy Aiyar, Presidential Address in the Psychology Conference. (Quoted from *Sri Aurobindo*, by A. B. Purani, p. 131)

[2] Ibid.

the Roman Forum; thousands of unexpected and mostly `undesirable' guests invade and trouble us. No inner activity can be seriously effective and continuous until we have first reduced our house to order, and then have recalled and reassembled our herd of scattered energies.
`The powers of the mind are like rays of dissipated light; when they are concentrated they illumine. This is the only means of Knowledge.' In all countries and at all times learned men, artists, great men of action or of intense meditation, have known and practiced it instinctively each in his own way, either consciously or subconsciously, as experience dictated. . . . The originality of Indian Raja-Yoga lies in the fact that it has been the subject for centuries past of a minutely elaborated experimental science for the conquest of concentration and mastery of the mind. By mind, the Hindu Yogi understands the instrument as well as the object of knowledge, and in what concerns the object, he goes very far, farther than I can follow him."[3]

Swami Vivekananda who is said to have personally perfected this yoga, has this to say:

"The science of Raja Yoga proposes to lay down before humanity a practical and scientifically worked-out method for reaching the truth."[4] Defending this unique yoga against the allegations of occult or esoteric, he says: ". . .There is no mystery in what I teach. . . .Anything that is secret and mysterious in these systems of yogas should be at once rejected. . . .Discard everything that weakens you. Mystery-mongering weakens the human brain. It has well-nigh destroyed Yoga - one of the grandest of sciences . . . . You must practice and see whether these things happen or not. . . .There is

---

[3] Romain Rolland, Life and Gospel of Vivekananda, p. 222

[4] Ibid. p. 222

III. Raja Yoga

neither mystery nor danger in it .... It is wrong to believe blindly."[5]

Through this yoga, after concerted practice, the practicant develops spiritual powers such as levitation, suspended animation, emanation of light, mind reading or clairvoyance. Although this phenomenon is a natural by-product of the spiritual exercise, it should not be misused or exhibited for gain or fame, but controlled for the ultimate benefit of the embodied self. Logically, the intense concentration of this power is what illumines a person into a dazzling lighthouse capable of removing darkness all around. Reproduced from the Gita are some shlokas which describe the methodology for engaging into the practice of Raja Yoga:

6.11-12   sucau dese pratisthapya sthiram asnam
atmanah n'atyucchritam n'atinicam cail'ajina-kus'ottaram. tatr'aikagram manah krtva yata-citt'endriya-kriyah, upavisy'asne yunjyad yogam atma-visuddhaye.

meaning: Let the sadhak, the practicant of this yoga, take his firm seat in a clean place, neither too high nor too low, covered with sacred grass and then a clean cloth over it, make his mind one-pointed and control his thoughts and senses for the purification of the soul.

6.13-14[6]

samam kaya-siro-grivam dharayann acalam sthirah
sampreksya nasik'agram svam

---

[5] Romain Rolland, <u>Life and Gospel of Vivekananda</u>, p. 226

शुचौ देशे प्रतिष्ठाप्य स्थिरमासनमात्मनः ।
नात्युच्छ्रितं नातिनीचं चैलाजिनकुशोत्तरम् ॥
तत्रैकाग्रं मनः कृत्वा यतचित्तेन्द्रियक्रियः ।
उपविश्यासने युञ्ज्याद्योगमात्मविशुद्धये ॥

[6] समं कायशिरोग्रीवं धारयन्नचलं स्थिरः । संप्रेक्ष्य नासिकाग्रं स्वं दिशश्चानवलोकयन् ॥
प्रशान्तात्मा विगतभीर्ब्रह्मचारिव्रते स्थितः । मनः संयम्य मच्चित्तो युक्त आसीत मत्परः ॥

. disasc'anavalokayan.
prasant'atma vigata-bhir brahmacari-vrate sthitah,
manah samyamya mac-citto yukta asita mat-parah

Meaning: Keeping his body, head and neck straight and his eyes fixed at the tip of his nose, without looking around, firm in celibacy (brahmacharya) and subdued in mind, let him sit harmonized with his mind turned to Me alone.

6.15-16[7] yunjannevam sada'tmanam yogi

niyata-manasah
santim nirvana-paramam mat-samstham
adhigacchati.
n'atyasnatas tu yogo 'sti na
c'aikantam anasnatah
na c'ati-svapna-silasya jagrato
n'aiva c'arjuna.

Meaning: Thus the yogin who has his mind controlled and his self harmonized attains to peace, the nirvana, which subsists in Me.

But this spiritual exercise is not verily for him who eats too much or abstains from eating too much; nor is it for him who sleeps too much, nor is it, O Arjuna, for him who does not sleep at all.

6.17[8]   yukt'ahara-viharasya yukta-cestasya

---

[7] युञ्जन्नेवं सदात्मानं योगी नियतमानसः । शान्ति निर्वाणपरमां मत्संस्थामधिगच्छति ॥
नात्यश्नतस्तु योगोऽस्ति न चैकान्तमनश्नतः । न चाति स्वप्नशीलस्य जाग्रतो नैव चार्जुन ॥

[8] युक्ताहारविहारस्य युक्तचेष्टस्य कर्मसु ।
युक्तस्वप्नावबोधस्य योगो भवति दुःखहा ॥

III. Raja Yoga

karmasu,
yukta-svapn'avabodhasya yoga bhavati
duhkha-ha.

Meaning: This yoga which destroys pain and suffering is for him who knows-the-mean in food and recreation, who knows-the-mean in doing the works, who knows-the-mean in sleeping and waking.

A detailed process is contained in Chapter 6 of the Gita, but it is summarized as follows:

To prepare for this yoga, the first thing to do is to select a proper place. The place is important because it is where the yogin has to do the meditation daily. The seat should be a flat untiltable floor or a wooden platform wide enough for a cross-legged sitting posture and overspread by a clean white cotton cloth or deerskin to enable the yogin to sit in concentration and, as his yoga progresses, to get lost in `samadhi' in course of time.

Technically, this yoga passes through eight stages:

I. Yama. This is the preparatory stage. The practicant begins seriously to control his desires, anger and undesirable mental flights. He has to take a vow to become a brahmchari, i.e., his sex life has to be controlled or regulated.

II. Niyama. He receives a structured program wherein he has to follow the basic rules of hygiene such as cleanliness, piety and pursuit of knowledge through study and contact and company with the saints and the seers well-versed in the religious practices and the yogas.

III.   Asana. He is now directed to select a spot for meditation which is called asana. The aim is to end activity, and get started into the meditation practice by a sitting posture. The place for the asana must be flat, untiltable which should be covered by a deerskin or a clean white cotton cloth. There he sits cross-legged, arms straight down resting over both knees.

IV.   Pratyahara. In this condition the mind controls all the senses and withdraws itself from all sense objects. If the mind tries to wander, as it usually does, it is subdued by the intellect. The Raja Yoga does not pamper the mind and allows it to have and enjoy whatever it desires, as the modern psychology does.

V.   Pranayama. This is the condition in which breath is regulated by means of breathing exercises. This is to produce emptiness in the mind in order to prepare for fixing the mind on a given point which is the first step in this meditation.

VI.   Dharana. In this stage the practicant forces the mind to stay on a certain point for as long as possible.

VII.   Dhayana. This is the meditation stage wherein the mind has attained an unbroken connection flowing toward the chosen point.

VIII.   Samadhi. This is the last stage in which the mind loses its consciousness; and the individual finds himself floating into the vastness of space. The individual merges with Totality and achieves a blissful comprehension of nothingness around him. He has lost his individuality and finds universality as long as he wants depending on the power he has so far achieved from his meditation. No words can describe this condition to the uninitiate and no intellect can formulate it; "through yoga must yoga be known."[9]

The exercises of Raja Yoga is not for the person who indulges in the extremes. The yogin must do all daily activities with moderation. He shouldn't eat too much nor should he eat too little or do the fasting; he should not sleep too much nor should he keep too much awake. `Yukta' is the most appropriate word in the Gita that describes this person. He `who-knows-the-mean' is the person most suited for this practice. This man has to be `moderate' as per samkra and `measured' as per Ramanuja, and `the same-and-indifferent' in all dualities. Besides, the yogin must learn to wait, persist and persevere where the going gets tough.

Arjuna was skeptical about the outcome of the Raja Yoga as claimed by Krishna; and therefore, he was candid in telling him of his doubts in the efficacy of this yoga since it is rather impossible to control the ever-wandering mind. Krishna admits that it is hard to control the mind as it is like controlling the wind, but he counsels Arjuna that all things are possible if pursued with devotion and dedication. The mind too can be controlled and brought to one-pointedness in meditation by continuous struggle. On Arjuna's further asking `what if the yogin fails to reach the goal', the Lord God advises him that `there is no sin or harm in not being able to succeed to the final stage of perfection or liberation as the yogin always gets the credit for whatever has been achieved, sooner or later, i.e., in this very life or in the lives to come! Here is what He says on this:

The blessed Lord said:

---

[9] Will Durant, Our Oriental Heritage, p. 544

6.40,41[10]

> Partha, n'aiv'eha n'anutra vinasas tasya vidyate:
> na hi kalyana-krt kascid durgatim, tata, gacchati.
> prapya punya-krtami lokan usitva sasvatih samah
> sucinam srimatam gehe yoga-bhrasto 'bhijayate.

Meaning: O'Partha, there is no destruction of such a person in this life or in any other future lives for no doer of right deeds misses the desired state. If he fails perfection, he will be born in a family of enlightened persons on exhausting his merit earned earlier or after enjoying even the pleasures of heaven if he had earned that stage in his earlier life.

6.43,45[11]

> tatra tam buddhi-samyogam labhate
> paurvadehikam,
> yatate ca tato bhuyah samsiddhau
> kuru-nandana.
> prayatnad yatamanas tu yogi
> samsuddha-kilbiash,
> aneka-janma-samsiddhas tato yati
> param gatim.

Meaning: There he regains the psychosomatic faculties (impressions of

---

[10] पार्थ नैवेह नामुत्र विनाशस्तस्य विद्यते ।
न हि कल्याणकृत्कश्चिद्दुर्गतिं तात गच्छति ॥
प्राप्य पुण्यकृतां लोकानुषित्वा शाश्वतीः समाः ।
[11] शुचीनां श्रीमतां गेहे योगभ्रष्टोऽभिजायते ॥
तत्र तं बुद्धिसंयोगं लभते पौर्वदेहिकम् ।
यतते च ततो भूयः संसिद्धौ कुरुनन्दन ॥

प्रयत्नाद्यतमानस्तु योगी संशुद्धकिल्बिषः ।
अनेकजन्मसंसिद्धस्ततो याति परां गतिम् ॥

perfection) which he had gathered in his previous lives and with those as the basis, he strives again for perfection, O Arjuna. But the Yogi who perseveres on while staying untainted through many many lives at last attains the highest estate, the nirvana.

And that is the fastest way it is for getting to the ultimate state of the Supreme Being without going through the sufferings of indefinite lives.

IV. BHAKTI YOGA

According to Goswami Tulsidas, "all dualities are the product of Nature (maya). They do not go away without worship of God. Therefore, he advises people to devote to His worship leaving all things aside."[1] Bhakti is the easiest, most popular and most recommended systems of all. Lord God Krishna Himself says this at the end of Chapter 6:

6.47[2] yoginam api sarvesam mad-
gaten'antaratmana
sraddhavan bhajate yo mam, sa me
yuktatamo matah.

Meaning: I believe that out of all the yogis the man who has faith in me and who loves and honors Me is absorbed in me the most.

Bhakti in Hinduism is not just worship in a temple. It is complete absorption in the quest for realization by whatever means possible. It is through knowledge, through good selfless deeds, through meditation or by all of the above together. Or it can be just what the person's own conscience may honestly suggest him to do for perfection, and to get united with the Supreme Being. Yet common man's bhakti requires selection of a deity from amongst the host of gods and goddesses popular in his society as the best manifestation of God's powers. Those who like abstract thinking in preference to idol worship, can meditate on Him as a formless Universal Being in the Arya Samaj style of Hinduism. In either case, whether with idol or without idol or

---

[1] —हरि माया कृत दोष गुन, बिनु हरि भजन न जाहिं ।
भजिअ राम तजि काम सब, अस बिचारि मन माहिं ॥१॥

[2] योगिनामपि सर्वेषां मद्गतेनान्तरात्मना ।
श्रद्धावान्भजते यो मां स मे युक्ततमो मतः ॥

picture, a form or shape of some kind, even of nothing, has to be formed. The bhakta, in the relationship with God, of master and servant, husband and wife, or beloved and lover or father and son, endeavors to establish union with the Supreme Being in complete surrender of his ego, his personal likes and dislikes and even his "I". His goal is reached when his self is completely absorbed with the Supreme Self and his individual identity is completely lost.

"Bhakti, in the Gita, is not an `amor intellectualis' which is more reflective and contemplative. It is sustained by knowledge but is not knowledge. It involves no reference to yoga technique or longing for speculative knowledge of the Divine. Sandilya argues that it gives us spiritual peace even without knowledge as in the case of milkmaids (Their love for Krishna). The devotee has a sense of utter humility. In the presence of the Ideal, he feels that he is nothing: God loves meekness, the utter prostration of the self."[3] The Lord God says this in the Gita and promises to liberate those who come to Him and Him alone:

18.65,66[4]   man-mana bhava mad-bhakto madyaji
mam namaskuru
mam ev'aisyasi, satyam te pratijane,
priyosime.

sarva-dharman parityajya mam ekam
saranam vraja:
aham tva sarva-papebhyo
moksayisyami, ma sucah.

---

[3]   S. Radhakrishnan, Bhagvadgita, p. 61

[4]   मन्मना भव मद्भक्तो मद्याजी मां नमस्कुरु ।
मामेवैष्यसि सत्यं ते प्रतिजाने प्रियोऽसि मे ॥

IV. Bhakti Yoga

Meaning: Fix your thoughts in Me, love Me and worship Me, do your sacrifice and prostration on to me: so you will come to Me. I promise you truly for you are dear to Me. (And, therefore) Give up all rules and rituals, turn to Me - your only refuge, for I will liberate you of all evils; have no worry.

In complete surrender to Him, the Lord God Krishna wants Arjuna to do His bidding in doing the fighting because this is his nature and also the dictate of the will of the Supreme Nature which none can resist. However, conceding to Arjuna his right to choose his options and never to surrender reason so characteristic of Hindu thought, the Lord God wants him to think over for himself in all its amplitude and "do whatever you will":

18.63[5] iti te jnanam akhyatam guhyad
guhyataram maya:
vimrsy'aitad asesena yath'ecchasi
tatha kuru.

Meaning: I have told you this, the most mysterious of all the mysterious wisdom. Now you do whatever you think proper pondering over all things in full amplitude.

Bhakti usually postulates effort on the part of the bhakta. This is likened to the ape way in which the young ape clings fast to the mother and is saved. There is, however, an aspect of bhakti, technically known as `prapatti' wherein no effort of the bhakta is needed. This is likened to the kitten way in which the mother cat takes the young in her mouth, the kitten making no effort whatsoever, and takes her into

---

[5] सर्वधर्मान्परित्यज्य मामेकं शरणं व्रज ।
अहं त्वा सर्वपापेभ्यो मोक्षयिष्यामि मा शुचः ॥
इति ते ज्ञानमाख्यातं गुह्याद्गुह्यतरं मया ।
विमृश्यैतदशेषेण यथेच्छसि तथा कुरु ॥

security. The difference lies perhaps in the intensity of the urge; but the practicant of Bhakti Yoga, being a thinking human, knows more how he would want to be saved.

A word of caution for the bhakta against the tendency to degenerate into morbid sentimentality. This happens in most uneducated work-shirking persons who little understand that bhakti too is as intelligent and conscientious a service as any other yoga with the exception that it is less technical than the others and it needs less systematic effort on the part of the bhakta. Some bhaktas tend to become imbeciles and escapees pretending that they themselves are to do nothing as the common working folk are there to do the work and serve them. In this category may be included those bhaktas - `sadhus' - who roam around the Indian streets especially in the holy places.

In the advanced stage of bhakti, the aspirant will be seeing all in one and one in all. He will begin seeing Him in the thing or person he likes best. Then, he will see Him in another, then in another, and afterwards, he will go on and on till he will find Him all over. Suppose, instead of beginning to worship a lower deity, he starts out with a higher deity or the God Almighty Himself, he has already gotten a head start in the realization of the goal. Obviously, the longer he will jump, the more ground will he cover. Greater is the reward for worshipping a greater being, the greatest for worshipping the greatest, the Absolute Being. The Lord God makes it amply clear in 7.23 of the Gita as mentioned earlier. "Faith (sraddha) is the basis of bhakti. So the gods in whom people have faith are tolerated. Some love is better than none, for if we do not love, we become shut up within ourselves. Besides, the lower gods are accepted as forms of the One Supreme. There is insistence on the fact that, while other devotees reach other ends, only he who is devoted to the Supreme reaches infinite bliss."[6]

---

[6] S. Radhakrishnan, Bhagvadgita, p. 64

Like aspirants of other yogas, the bhakta too, in the process of realization, reaches a point when he bursts into a unique ecstasy in which he gets into away-from-the-ordinary life. He has shed forms and symbols of a religious denomination; and no church or temple binds him or interests him. All places are churches or temples; and all living beings are gods or God's beings for him. He has become One with all. There is no `you' and no `me' for him as he sees all in One and One in all. "Bhakti leads to jnana or wisdom. For Ramanuja, it is smrtisantana. Even `prapatti' is a form of jnana. When the devotion glows, the Lord dwelling in the soul imparts to the devotee by His grace the light of wisdom. The devotee feels united intimately with the Supreme, who is experienced as the being in whom all antitheses vanish. He sees God in himself and himself in God. Prahlada says that the Supreme end for man is absolute devotion to God and a feeling of His presence everywhere. `For her who loves, it is the same whether she, in the ardor of love, plays on the bosom of the lover or whether she caresses with tenderness his feet. Thus to him who knows, whether he remain in a superconscious ecstasy or serves God with worship, the two are the same.'"[7] "When the last stage has been reached, you will no longer need to know what is going to happen to you, or if God, the creator of the universe, an almighty and pitiful God, a God who rewards the merits of humanity, exists, it will not matter to you even if God is tyrant or a good God....`The lover has passed beyond all these - beyond rewards and punishments, beyond fears, or doubts, or scientific or any other demonstration...."[8]

---

[7] S. Radhakrishnan, <u>Bhagvadgita</u>, p. 64
[8] Romain Rolland, <u>Life and Gospel of Vivekananda</u>, p.217

SHIVA IN ETERNAL MOVEMENT

SYMBOLIZING

ETERNALLY CHANGING

UNIVERSE

NATURE'S ETERNAL RELIGION

"The absence of a common body of doctrine puzzles those Westerners who study Hinduism assuming that it is a religion," says Troy Wilson Organ. They find in Hinduism an object of belief like they do in Christianity or Islam. To Organ, Hindu thought is not a philosophy. It is "a philosophical religion .... The existential flavor of Hindu sadhna so pervades the entire corpus of its writings and practices that existentialism has never arisen as a protest movement against essentialism.... The more exact method is to affirm that Hinduism is a sadhna which seeks to guide man to integration, to spiritualization, and to liberation.... The concept of reincarnation is the Hindu way of asserting that there are no temporal nor developmental limits to the perfecting."[1] Hindu thought is natural, reasonable, and scientific. It needs no cover up or improvement or rationalizing. It has stayed the same during the ongoing scientific inquiry in almost all sociological aspects. It never filled up the holes to make its religious stories look reasonable or believable. In the Hindu Monism (Advaita) God is not anthropomorphic being. He is the All; and there is no one different from Him that can be called sinner and be punished, or be called faithful and be loved and saved. He is not a despot or autocratic God. There is no question of his loving or hating any one part more than the others; and in the same manner, unless He is a dictator, He should not require allegiance or faith from any one. However, as the living beings in the society became diverse and different and graded, certain living beings, humans especially, respected, adored, and worshipped the better human beings with love and faith that each one of them deserved depending upon the services these better humans rendered to the society and got themselves known as devas (gods) which actually means `the givers'. These better men and women were elevated as gods and goddesses to

---

[1] Troy Wilson Organ, <u>The Hindu Quest for the Perfection of Man,</u> p. 5

give the structure and tangibility to human virtues that the society needed from its components. The Greeks have had a similar institution of gods and goddesses before it was smothered by the Christian dogma.

The greatest surviving feature of Hinduism has been its positive ideas not meant for the followers of any particular religion or race. Hinduism is not, in fact, a religion in the sense of the western religions so that those not belonging to it are infidels or heretics. It states the truth and teaches need for work to attain perfection for salvation, not just faith and `no work'. It needs no worshippers to worship its God, because it has no God different from the God of the people of other religions. It has been encouraging its own followers to try to worship the God in the manner other people do unlike the `saints' of other religions who must insist that their own `God'and their `manner' of worship is the best and acceptable way to God. Nanak, Kabir, Dadu, and Ramakrishna Paramhamsa are well-known Hindu saints who have been practicing Hinduism with other religions.

Hinduism has not approved proselytism as a means of increasing the number of its adherents. Even religious propaganda is discouraged because truth needs no trumpeting. It has always relied upon the positive nature of its philosophy. Proselytism was tried by Buddhism, but after a phenomenal success in the past, it failed; and it failed Buddhism too. It was tried by Rishi Dayananda in Hinduism on a short scale, but it had to be abandoned due to the negative nature of the program. Therefore, Hindu saints and seers have been dead set against converting people to their religions. Instead, they advise people to free themselves from the shackles of dogmas, bigotry, and anger, and find truth wherever it is seen. During the bitterest days of pre-Independence India, Mahatma Gandhi was reportedly approached by a non-Hindu for converting himself to Hinduism. The Mahatma chided the young man, and advised him to stay where he was, as all religions are good.

Hinduism has been interpreted to the modern world by many Hindu intellectuals who were educated through the medium of English. The interpretation of each of them is different in manner and style, but the content of their version of the Hindu thought is the same - undogmatic, free, and universally human, and accepting all mankind, hating none on any ground. In fact, since Hinduism is scientific and progressive, they have shown to the world the human ideal of super conscient man or universal mind to be pursued as the individual and collective goal of all humans away from the funny childish dogma of sin, superstition, fear, false hope, or damnation that continues to retard progress. Following are the personal statements of five great Hindus of modern India, who have seen the dynamic Hinduism steer India out of its age long poverty, ignorance and superstition, born out of her political subjugation, into the proud strong independent India of today.

यं ब्रह्मा वरुणेन्द्ररुद्रमरुतः स्तुन्वन्ति दिव्यैः स्तवै-
र्वेदैः साङ्गपदक्रमोपनिषदैर्गायन्ति यं सामगाः ।
ध्यानावस्थिततद्गतेन मनसा पश्यन्ति यं योगिनो
यस्यान्तं न विदुः सुरासुरगणा देवाय तस्मै नमः ॥

Rabindranath Tagore
PREDICTED INDIA'S RESURGENCE BY LOVING WESTERN SCIENTIFIC AND TECHNOLOGICAL IDEAS AS WELL AS HER OWN PHILOSOPHIES.

RABINDRANATH TAGORE
(1861 - 1941)

Rabindranath Tagore was the son of Debindranath Tagore, a follower of Raja Ram Mohan Roy, who attempted to bring new life into India by simultaneously returning to the sources of the Hindu tradition and turning to the West. He continued intimate connections with Brahmo Samaj of which his father was a staunch supporter. Deeply patriotic, he did not believe in the narrow nationalism that political leaders of the then Indian National Congress were indulging into. That is why he was not very active in supporting the movement. A narrow, parochial Indian nationalism, he believed, would come in the way of a new order of civilization and culture of the world that independent India was destined to bring about. He was a great poet and philosopher and won for himself a Nobel Prize in Literature which gave him enormous prestige all over the world and ultimately made him one of the most respected professors of the universal character of Hindu tradition. He envisioned a very rapid diffusion of Hinduism all over through India's intimate relationship with the West which he states as under in a very prophetic manner:

.The Englishman has come through the breach in our crumbling walls, as the messenger of the Lord of the world festival, to tell us that the world has need of us; not where we are petty, but where we can help with the force of our Life, to rouse the World in wisdom, love and work, in the expansion of insight, knowledge and mutuality. . . .The India to which the Englishman has come with his message, is the India which is shooting up towards the future from within the bursting seed of the past. This new India belongs to humanity. What right have we to say who shall and who shall not find a place therein. Who is this "We"? Bengali, Marathi or Panjabi, Hindu or Mussalman? Only the larger "We" in whom all these - Hindu, Moslem and Englishman, and whosoever else there be - may eventually unite shall have the right to dictate who is to remain and who is to leave.

On us today is thrown the responsibility of building up this greater India, and for that purpose our immediate duty is to justify our meeting with the Englishman. It shall not be permitted to us to say that we would rather remain aloof, inactive, irrresponsive, unwilling to give and to take, and thus to make poorer the India that is to be." He envisions a heaven of freedom and truth for all mankind where there is no fear, no frictions, no ignorance, but people living by reason, and India being a part of that whole universal culture. He sums up this vision into the following poem from his famous creation `Geetanjali':

INTO THAT HEAVEN OF FREEDOM

Where the mind is without fear
and the head is held high,
Where knowledge is free;
Where the world has not been broken
up into fragments by narrow domestic
walls;
Where words come out from the
depth of truth;
Where tireless striving
stretches its arms towards
perfection;
Where the clear stream of reason

> has not lost its way into the
> dreary desert sand of dead habit;
> Where the mind is led forward
> by thee into ever-widening
> thought and action —
> Into that heaven of freedom,
> my Father,
> let my country awake.
>
> *Rabindranath Tagore*
>
> Santiniketan

LET MY COUNTRY AWAKE.

VIVEKANANDA
THE HINDU SAINT OF POWER

"CHRISTS AND BUDDHAS ARE BUT WAVES ON THE BOUNTLESS OCEAN WHICH I AM."

SWAMI VIVEKANANDA
(1863 - 1904)

The prophet who, according to Rabindranath Tagore, was destined to introduce Hinduism to the West and rehabilitate India as the land of primeval thought was none but his fellow Bengalee in his own age group known at that time as Narendranath Dutta, but known later, all over the world as Vivekananda. This young man became the beloved hero of all Indians of every rank and file, accomplished the assignment given to him by his master within a short period of less than ten years, and like the great Shankracharya, who returned to his heavenly abode at the age of twenty-eight years upon establishing the four dhamas (monastries) on the four corners of India, consumed himself through the incessant work of uplifting India, at the very young age of forty.

Educated through the medium of English and well-versed in the sciences, Naren, as he was lovingly called by his master, Ramakrishna Paramhamsa, was skeptical about the traditional Hinduism; but in his master, whom he met by chance, he happened to experience illimitable spiritual powers which shook him off his feet and fired him to undertake the mission that his master entrusted him with. Therefore, like a hungry lion in search of a prey, he searched the whole of India for men and material with which to build a program so he could devour everything that afflicted his dear India and Hinduism, and raise her to the position of the leader of the world, which she deserved, until at last he reached at the Parliament of Religions in Chicago to settle scores with the leaders of the other religions of the world.

He went, he saw, he conquered. "When this quite unknown young man of thirty appeared in Chicago at the inaugural meeting of the Parliament of Religions, opened in September 1893 by Cardinal Gibbons, all his fellow-members were forgotten in his commanding presence. His strength and beauty, the grace and dignity of his bearing, the dark light of his eyes, his imposing appearance, and from the moment he began to speak, the splendid music of his rich, deep voice enthralled the vast audience of American Anglo-Saxons, previously prejudiced against him on account of his color. The thought of this warrior prophet of India left a deep mark upon the United States. . . .He was a born king and nobody ever came near him either in India or America without paying homage to his majesty."[1] Therefore, he gave right and left to all who made mockery of religion and commanded all his countrymen, big and small, high and low into the task of nation building. His message was karma - work and work, unselfish and unattached - the same message that Lord Krishna gave to the despondent Arjuna at the battlefield of Kurukshetra:

"Above all, be strong, be manly! I have a respect even for one who is wicked, so long as he is manly and strong; for his strength will make him some day give up his wickedness or even give up all work for selfish ends, and will then eventually bring him into the Truth."[2]

"Strength, virile reason, constant preoccupation with universal good and complete disinterestedness are the conditions for reaching the goal. And there is still another: it is the will to arrive. Most men who call themselves religious are not really so at bottom; they are too lazy, too fearful, too insincere; they prefer to linger on the way and not to look too closely at what is awaiting them; hence they stagnate in the lotus land of formal devotion. 'Temples or churches, books or forms are just for the child's play, so as to make the spiritual man strong enough to take yet higher steps, and these first steps are necessary to be taken if he wants religion'".[3] And a true rationalistic religion is needed now

---

[1] Romain Roilland, Life and Gospel of Vivekananda, p.5

[2] Ibid. p.4

[3] Romain Rolland, Life and Gospel of Vivekananda, p. 194

more than ever before. "The salvation of Europe depends on a rationalistic religion. And such a religion exists; it is the Advaita of India, Non-Dualism, Unity, the idea of the Absolute, of the Impersonal God, the only religion that can have any hold on intellectual people. The Advaita has twice saved India from materialism. By the coming of Buddha, who appeared in a time of most hideous and widespread materialism.... By the coming of Samkara, who when materialism had reconquered India in the form of the demoralization of the governing classes and of superstition in the lower orders, put fresh life into Vedanta, by making a rational philosophy emerge from it."[4]

True to the philosophy of Hinduism, Vivekananda advocated the divine in all living beings as he said his eternal words: "Never forget the glory of human nature! We are the greatest God...Christs and Buddhas are but waves on the bountless ocean which I AM."[5]

---

[4]   Ibid, p. 259

[5]   Ibid, p. 177

AUROBINDO GHOSE

The man is gradually evolving to be superman.

AUROBINDO GHOSE
(1872 - 1950)

With faith in Raja-yoga, and just to accelerate the human liberation bypassing the doctrines of Jnana and Karma Yogas, Yogiraj Aurobindo took to spiritual exercises to eliminate discord and disequilibrium from matter and spirit in order to obtain divine life for the human race. He visualized a conscient man, a superman in further evolution of man's development just as man himself is the next higher stage from his previous animal stage. A superhuman ideal postulated superhuman effort for man which he took early in life and continued until his death in 1950. I wish Aurobindo had an immortal body to fulfil the task.

He was born in a Bengalee home of upper middle-class parents who sent him to England for higher education from where he returned to enter the Indian Civil Service, a prized career for the Indians of those days. Contrary to all expectations, he soon quit his lucrative job and entered politics and became an aggressive worker of the Indian National Congress, which was not the style of the Congress of those days. As apprehended, he was picked up by the British Government and was accused of advocating terrorism and violence. The politics of those days did not satisfy his ambition for his country and the human race. So, he dramatically withdrew from all activity and retired to Pondicherry, a small town in South India, to devote himself exclusively to the pursuit of yoga in the ancient Hindu way. His philosophy of supermind is stated thus:

".... We speak of the evolution of life in Matter, the evolution of Mind in Matter, but evolution is a word which merely states the phenomenon without explaining it. For there seems to be no reason why life should evolve out of material elements or Mind out of living form, unless we accept the Vedantic solution that life is already involved in

Matter and Mind in Life because in essence Matter is a form of veiled Life, Life a form of veiled Consciousness. And then there seems to be little objection to a further step in the series and the admission that mental consciousness may itself be only a form and a veil of higher states which are beyond Mind. In that case, the unconquerable impulse of man toward God, Light, Bliss, Freedom, Immortality presents itself in its right place in the chain as simply the imperative impulse by which Nature is seeking to evolve beyond Mind, and appears to be as natural, true and just as the impulse toward Life which she has planted in certain forms of Matter or the impulse toward Mind which she has implanted in certain forms of Life. As there, so here, the impulse exists more or less obscurely in her different vessels with an ever-ascending series in the power of its will-to-be; a there, so here, it is gradually evolving and bound fully to evolve the necessary organs and faculties. As the impulse toward Mind ranges from the more sensitive reactions of Life in the metal and plant up to its full organization in man, so in man himself there is the same ascending series, the preparation, if nothing more, of a higher and divine life. The animal is a living laboratory in which Nature has, it is said, worked out man. Man himself may be a thinking and living laboratory in whom and with whose conscious cooperation she wills to work out the superman, the god. Or shall we not say, rather, to manifest God? For if evolution is the progressive manifestation by Nature of that which slept or worked in her, involved, it is also the overt realization of that which she secretly is. We cannot, then, bid her pause at a given stage of her evolution, nor have we the right to condemn with the religionist as perverse and presumptuous or with the rationalist as a disease or hallucination any intention she may evince or effort she may make to go beyond. If it be true that Spirit is involved in Matter and apparent Nature is secret God, then the manifestation of the divine in himself and the realization of God within and without are the highest and most legitimate aim possible to man upon earth."[1]

---

[1] Aurobindo Ghose, The Life Divine, pp 1-7

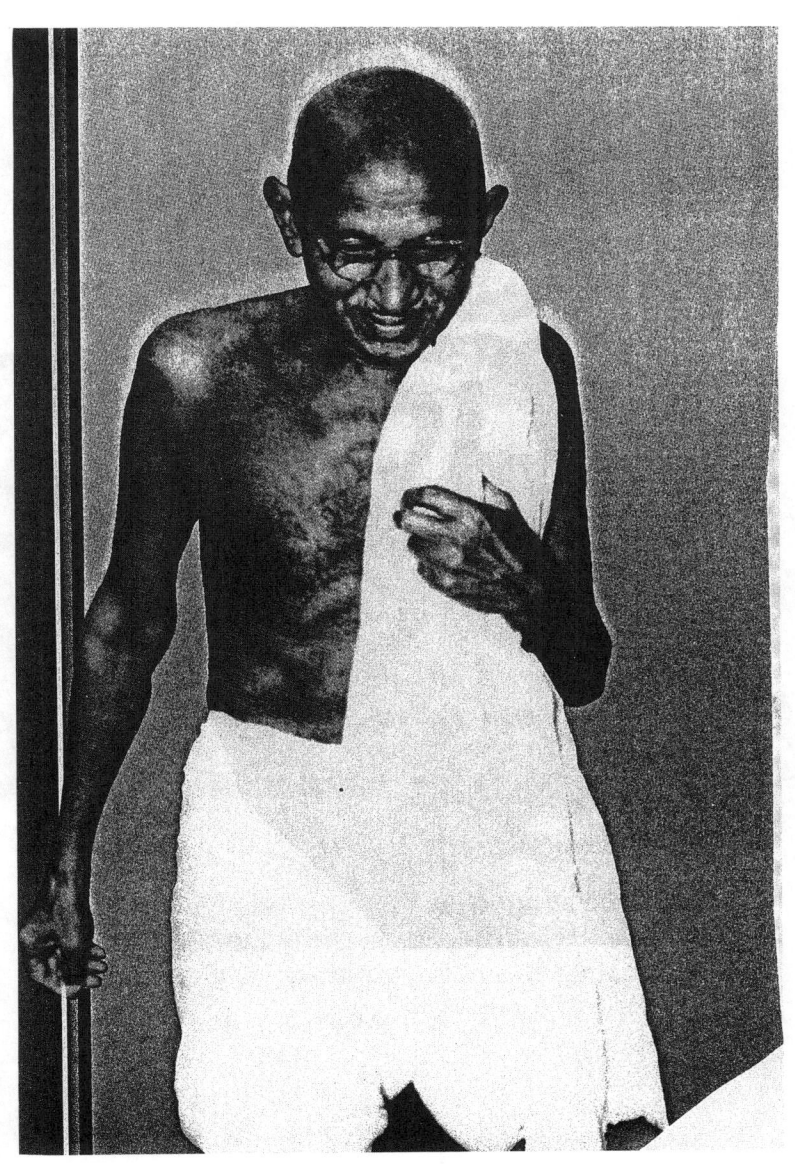

NEHRU WITH GANDHI

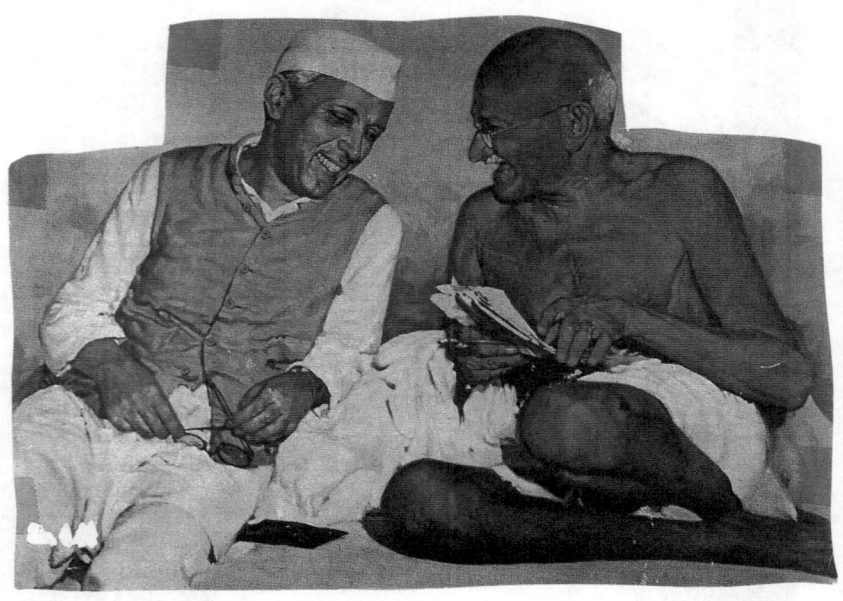

One of the greatest intellectuals of his time in full humility learning at the feet of the master whose qualification was nothing but the whole Truth.

MAHATMA GANDHI
(1869 - 1948)

Albert Einstein said: "Generations to come will scarcely believe that such the one as this ever, in flesh and blood, walked upon this earth"; and General George C. Marshall, the then American Secretary of State added: "Mahatma Gandhi has become the spokesman of the conscience of all mankind. He was a man who made humility a simple truth more powerful than the empires." Yes, Mahatma Gandhi was a private man, `without wealth, without property, without official title or office. He was not the commander of armies, nor the ruler of vast lands. He could not boast any scientific achievement or artistic gift, yet when he died, millions of men, governments and dignitaries from all over the world swarmed Delhi to pay homage to this little brown man in loin cloth' who led his country to freedom just by counseling the most powerful kingdom into justice.

Jawaharlal Nehru, his chief disciple, who did not believe God, believed Gandhi more than anybody else, and said of his master that wherever on earth Gandhi traveled that land became holy with his contact. It is by contact with Gandhi that this one of the greatest of the modern Indian intellectuals gave up his princely estates and gladly lived in the British Indian jails with him for decades. No wonder some of his countrymen wanted to worship Gandhi in a temple but were dissuaded from doing so on being told of Gandhi's views on deification.

The story of Gandhi's life should be well-known to almost all the literate people of the world and, therefore, needs no summarization. Building upon the work of previous reformers, but chiefly relying on his own genius, Gandhi gave the Indian independence movement a uniqueness. His ahimsa, non-violence, was a positive weapon of the weak and the poor against the strong and the rich. He drew freely from western philosophers, and Ruskin and Tolstoy were his favorite readings; but he stayed firmly grounded in the fundamentals of Hindu Sanatan Dharma taking constant inspiration from the Ramayana of Goswami Tulsidas and Shrimad Bhagvadgita whom he called the mother. He was more concerned about means which would justify his ends. He called his autobiography as Experiments with Truth as he candidly told therein all which no ordinary person would tell about his life for fear of guilt or embarrassment. He remained true to his convictions till the time of his assassination by a person who did not like his love for the enemies of his people and his country. His interpretation of the philosophy of Hinduism is summarized as under:

"In Hinduism, incarnation is ascribed to one who has performed some extraordinary service to mankind. All embodied life is in reality an incarnation of God, but it is not usual to consider every living being an incarnation. Future generations pay this homage to one who, in his own generation, has been extraordinarily religious in his conduct. I can see nothing wrong in this procedure; it takes nothing from God's greatness, and there is no violence done to Truth. There is an Urdu saying which means, `Adam is not God, but he is a spark of Divine.' And, therefore, he who is the most religiously behaved has the most of the divine spark in him. It is in accordance with this train of thought that Krishna enjoys, in Hinduism, the status of the most perfect incarnation.

This belief in incarnation is a testimony of man's lofty spiritual ambition. Man is not at peace with himself till he has become like unto God. The endeavor to reach this state is the supreme, the only ambition worth having. And this self-realization is the subject of the Gita, as it is of all the scriptures. But the author of the Gita surely did not write it to establish that doctrine. The object of the Gita appears to me to be that of showing the most excellent way to attain self-realization. That which is to be found, more or less clearly, spread out here and there in Hindu religious books, has been brought out in the clearest possible language in the Gita even at the risk of repetition.

THAT MATCHLESS REMEDY IS RENUNCIATION OF FRUIT OF ACTION:

This is the center around which the Gita is woven. This renunciation is the central sun, around which devotion, knowledge, and the rest revolve like planets. The body has been likened to a prison. There must be action where there is body. Not one embodied being is exempted from labor. And yet all religions proclaim that it is possible for man, by treating the body as the temple of God, to attain freedom. Every action is tainted, be it ever so trivial. How can the body be made the temple of God? In other words, how can one be free from action, i.e., from the taint of sin? Gita has answered the question in decisive language: `By desireless action; by renouncing fruits of action; by dedicating all activities to God, i.e., by surrendering oneself to Him, body and soul. This is the unmistakable teaching of the Gita. He who gives up action falls. He who gives up only the reward rises. But renunciation of fruit in no way means indifference to the result. In regard to every action one must know the result that is expected to follow, the means thereto, and the capacity for it. He, who, being thus equipped, is without desire for the result and is yet wholly engrossed in the due fulfillment of the task before him is said to have renounced the fruit of his action.

Again let no one consider renunciation to mean want of fruit for the renouncer. The Gita reading does not warrant such a meaning. Renunciation means absence of hankering after fruit. As a matter of fact, he who renounces reaps a thousand fold. The renunciation of the Gita is the acid test of faith. He who is ever brooding over result often loses nerve in the performance of his duty. He becomes impatient and then gives vent to anger and begins to do unworthy things; he jumps from action to action never remaining faithful to any. He who broods over result is like a man given to objects of senses; he is ever distracted, he says goodbye to all scruples, to means fair and foul to attain his end.... Thinking along these lines, I have felt that in trying to enforce in one's life the central teaching of the Gita, one is bound to follow Truth and ahimsa. When there is no desire for fruit, there is no temptation for untruth or ahimsa. Take any instance of untruth or violence, and it will be found that at its back was the desire to attain the cherished end."[1]

RIGHT CONDUCT:

(THE GUIDE FOR RIGHTEOUSNESS IS YOUR OWN MANAH (FREE MIND).

---

[1] Mahatma Gandhi, in Desai, <u>The Gita According to Gandhi</u>, pp. 128 - 32

NONVIOLENCE
IS THE ONLY CHOICE FOR THE SURVIVAL OF THE HUMAN RACE

DR. SARVEPALLI RADHAKRISHNAN
SECOND PRESIDENT OF INDIA
WORLD FAMOUS MODERN AUTHORITY ON HINDU THOUGHT

SARVEPALLI RADHAKRISHNAN
(1888 - 1975)

Quite like a rishi of the ancient times in acquiring wisdom and dispensing it all over, and admittedly a well-known authority on Indian metaphysics, Dr. Radhakrishnan was born in a Brahman family of south India (Andhra Pradesh) on September 5, 1888. He crowned a career of academic distinction and was honored to become the Vice Chancellor of Benaras Hindu University and later the Spalding Professor of Eastern Religions at Oxford. On return from England, he successively became free India's Ambassador to the USSR, Vice President of India in 1952, and her President in 1962. He died in Madras on April 17, 1975.

Learned in Sanskrit and English alike, he was one of the best interpreters of the Hindu thought to the English speaking people all over the world. He lived in England for a long time and had deep and intimate knowledge of the English language, ways and manners; yet he stayed a thoroughly orthodox Hindu in his dress, eating habits, demeanor and disposition. He wore a turban in the south Indian style and wore his traditional dhoti (Indian loin cloth), the symbol of Indian common man and of course of Hindu erudition, which he never abandoned even when Indian intellectuals thought it an honor and a mark of high status to dress like an English man. Out of such a personality has come a statement of Hindu metaphysics expressed with power, passion and persuasion which was uniquely his, and proved the point that true knowledge is power, and it can be the highest temporal power since by virtue of his wisdom and work, he was chosen to become the President of India.

Hinduism is not just a faith to Radhakrishnan; it is the union of reason and intuition that cannot be defined but is only to be experienced. He spoke not just interpreting the scriptures of the Hindus but telling and teaching the people all over as if they were his pupils, about the real truth in the matter of religion. The following sampling of his interpretation illustrates the deftness of his presentation:

"We are now at the end of our course. We see that the Hindu recognizes one supreme spirit, though different names are given to it. In his social economy he has many castes, but one society. In the population there are many races and tribes, but all are bound together by one common spirit. Though many forms of marriage are permitted, there is only one ideal aimed at. There is a unity of purpose underlying the multitudinous ramifications. It may perhaps be useful to conclude this course with a brief resume of the central spirit of Hinduism and its application to the problems of religion and society.

The world which is a perpetual flow is not all. Its subjection to law and tendency to perfection indicate that it is based on a spiritual reality which is not exhausted in any particular object or group of objects. God is in the world; though not <u>as</u> the world. His creative activity is not confined to the significant stages in the evolutionary process. He does not merely intervene to create life or consciousness, but is working continuously. There is no dualism of the natural and the supernatural. The spiritual is an emergent of the natural in which it is rooted. The Hindu spirit is that attitude toward life which regards the endless variety of the visible and the temporal world as sustained and supported by the invisible and eternal spirit.

Evil, error and ugliness are not ultimate. Evil has reference to the distance which good has to traverse. Ugliness is half-way to beauty. Error is a stage on the road to truth. They have all to be outgrown. No view is so utterly erroneous, no man is so absolutely evil as to deserve complete castigation. If one human soul fails to reach its divine destiny, to that extent the universe is a failure. As every soul is unlike all others in the world, the destruction of even the most wicked soul will create void in God's scheme. There is no Hell, for that means there is a place where God is not, and there are sins which exceed his love. If the infinite love of God is not a myth, universal salvation is a certainty. But until it is achieved, we shall have error and imperfection. In a continuously evolving universe evil and error are inevitable, though they are gradually diminishing.

In religion, Hinduism takes it stand on a life of spirit, and affirms that the theological expressions of religious experience are bound to be varied. One metaphor succeeds another in the history of theology until God is felt as the central reality in the life of man and the world. Hinduism repudiates the belief resulting from a dualistic attitude that the plants in may garden are of God, while those in my neighbor's are weeds planted by the Devil which we should destroy at any cost. On the principle that the best is not the enemy of the good, Hinduism accepts all forms of belief and lifts them to a higher level. The cure for error is not the stake or the cudgel, not force or persecution, but the quiet diffusion of light.

In practical religion, Hinduism recognizes that there are those who wish to see God face to face, others who delight in the endeavor to know the truth of it all. Some find peace in action, others in non-action. A comprehensive religion guides each along his path to the common goal. We must not give supreme and sole importance to our specialty. Perfection can be attained as a celibate, or a householder, or an anchorite. A rigid uniform outlook is wrong. The saintliness of the holy man does not render the steadfastness of the devoted wife or the simple innocence of the child superfluous. The perfection of every type is divine. 'Whatsoever is glorious, good, beautiful and mighty, understand that it goes forth from out of a fragment of my splendor.'

The law of Karma tells us that the individual life is not a term, but a series. Fresh opportunities will be open to us until we reach the end of the journey. The historical forms we assume will depend on our work in the past. Heaven and Hell are higher and lower stages in one continuous movements. They are not external to the experiencing individuals. Purification is by means of purgation. The wages of sin is suffering. We need not regard sin as original and virtue as vicarious. We should do our duty in that state of life to which we happen to be called. Most of us have not a free hand in selecting our vocation. Freedom consists in making the best of what we have, our parentage, our physical nature and mental gifts. Every kind of capacity, every form of vocation, if rightly used, will lead us to the center.... No one can be at the same time a perfect saint, a perfect artist, and a perfect philosopher. Every definite type is limited by boundaries which deprive it of other possibilities. The worker should realize his potentialities through his work, and should perform it in a spirit of service to the commonweal. Work is craftsmanship and service. Our class conflicts are due to the fact that a warm living sense of unity does not bind together the different groups.

There has been no such thing as a uniform, stationary, unalterable Hinduism whether in point of belief or practice. Hinduism is a movement, not a position; process, not a result; a growing tradition, not a fixed revelation. Its past history encourages us to believe that it will be found equal to any emergency that the future may throw up, whether on the field of thought or of history.... We feel that our society is in a condition of unstable equilibrium. There is much wood that is dead and diseased that has to be cleared away. Leaders of Hindu thought and practice are convinced that the times require, not a surrender of the basic principles of Hinduism, but a restatement of them.... Such an attempt will only be the repetition of a process which has occurred a number of times in the history of Hinduism. The work of readjustment is in process. Growth is slow when roots are deep. But those who light a little candle in the darkness will help to make the whole sky aflame."

(S. Radhakrishnan, The Hindu Way of Life, pp. 124 - 30)

WARS TO ESTABLISH THE RULE OF DHARMA

THE EPICS

The two epics of which Hinduism is proud are the Ramayana and the Mahabharata. Both took shape in pre-Buddhistic period. Rishi Valmiki is the author of the Ramayana, and the Mahabharata is was written by Bhagwan Ved Vyasa. Both have essentially the same moral that it is the good or the right which ultimately prevails not the evil or the wrong. If the Ramayana is an ethical poem whose characters are duty bound to do what is right, the Mahabharata is a comprehensive drama mirroring practical people with their natural prides, prejudices, egos, and ideals.

Jules Michelet, the French historian, has said this in 1864 about the Ramayana: "Whoever has done or willed too much let him drink from this deep cup a long draught of life and youth .... Everything is narrow in the West - Greece is small and I stifle; Judea is dry and I pant. Let me look toward lofty Asia, and the profound East for a little while. There lies my great poem, as vast as the Indian ocean, blessed, gilded with the sun, the book of divine harmony wherein is no dissonance. A serene peace reigns there, and in the midst of conflict an infinite sweetness, a boundless fraternity, which spreads over all living things, an ocean (without bottom or bound) of love, of pity, of clemency."[1]

The Ramayana is the story of the members of a royal family who act in time of adversity with right conduct which becomes example for members of any family in any part of the world. It shows the ideal character of a brother, a wife, a father, a citizen or of a righteous person like Vibhikshana who denounced and parted his elder brother Ravana's company because he was evil. Rama is shown an

---

[1] Quoted from Jawaharlal Nehru, Discovery of India, p. 96

ideal king in peace and war. Upon defeating Ravana, he does not take his country not does he rob his treasury or mistreat his people, but returns the rule to Ravana's surviving younger brother Vibhikshna. Even the evil Kekai is reformed when Rama, the victim and all other members of the family do not hate and retaliate against her, but win her over by attributing her wrongs due to the influence of Karma.

The poet Ved Vyasa of the Mahabharata has depicted a real society like a fabric woven with both white and black threads, and a lot of corrective lectures for social amends. Again and again we come to philosophical teachings in this massive book which is seven times equal to the Iliad and the Odyssey together, and that is not all, the poet has taken out the essence, the cream of the Mahabharata, and put it in a small poetry book, popularly known as the Bhagvadgita which, in the poet's own words, is a summary and substitute for all the scriptures.

Rishi Ved Vyasa who had foreseen, and then personally witnessed the entire drama of the war with his own eyes and put it down in writing wanted to re-establish the rule of righteousness through the intervention of Lord God incarnate, Krishna, emphasizing the fact that in this world nothing happens without His will; and humans and super humans, gods or demigods, have no power to obstruct His processes. Their egos, and wrong deeds are born out of their ignorance of and attachment to the things material (maya) that deludes them. The solution lies in trying to see through the things by jnana, karma, atmasayyam and bhakti as explained in the Gita. The goal should not be acquisition of powers or possessions as was sought by Duryodhana, but liberation (mukti) through dharma - the righteous conduct, as shown by the Pandavs under the guidance of Lord Krishna. Beside resolving the philosophical questions, the poet has moralized on almost all mundane situations, some of which of our common knowledge are:

That lust, anger, greed and attachment (kam, krodh, lobh and moh, respectively) are the gateway to hell. The wise should try to shed them. Even Lord Krishna, incarnated as a human, was shaken in his resolve under the influence of anger.

That parents who fail to teach obedience and right conduct to the children have to grieve like Dhritrashtra did.

That when brothers fight, they ruin the family, even the empire that they belong. United they are strong, divided they are weak.

That the virtuous character is the real power and greatest wealth, even in adversity.

That the society which fails to respect its women perishes because the women are not the sex objects of any person or president of the persons.

That blind obedience is ruinous to the one who submits to it. It is slavery and sinful.

That addiction to gambling or any vice, such as, smoking, drinking or drugs is ruinous to the persons addicted and later to the society.

That injustice and hungry people are the source of unrest and ultimate war. The people cannot be deprived of their natural equal rights.

That the honorable men must have moral courage to stand against injustice even if it means losing their power, position, livelihood, or life.

That the war must be avoided, if at all possible, as it ruins the vanquished and the victor both. The all knowledgeable poet Ved Vyasa had the premonition of the possibility of a cosmic doom through atomic war when he hinted to non-violence as our only choice on seeing Ashwatthama and Arjuna poised at each other with their respective Pashupat Astras which, if not withdrawn at the command of the Rishi, would have destroyed the whole world.

That the truth triumphs ultimately and love humbles all.

That God is another name of the all-powerful cosmic machine of nature, the cause-and-effect mechanism, the karma, whose wheel moves on in accordance with its own Moral Order.

That man is an infinitesimal part of God and is merely a pawn moved by His all-powerful Will which no man or god can resist or thwart. His salvation lies in accepting his limited position and working without attachment to this transient material world.

The Mahabharata is a fathomless mine of the illimitable varieties of precious stones in the form of philosophical truths. One can find whatever one likes and wants. It is not a sectarian book, and is for all mankind. It has been a treasure house of thought and all thinkers, including Westerners, from Homer to Huxley, have been taking away whatever gems of thought they wanted. Through Lord Krishna's lecture to Arjuna contained in the Bhagvadgita, the poet has focussed, among others, on two main issues: one, that the embodied self is immortal because it is a minute part of God. It is never born and it never dies. It travels independently on its voyage transmigrating from body to body until it attains perfection and merges with the parent soul, the paramatma. The other is the importance of Karma, the human work. Even though work is important as all humans have to work because none can live without working, the work good or bad binds. Evil act is wrong and degrades the soul without doubt, but the day to day normal human acts also bind the soul to the material objects. A chain whether of gold or iron binds by its very nature. The more a person acquires, the more is he possessed by Maya, and is removed farther away from moksha which is the soul's ultimate destination. It is, therefore, suggested that work should not be done with selfish motive or with an eye on the fruits of the work. When the work is done in the spirit of worklessness or done as a sacrifice without even an expectation of the result of it is right work that truly integrates and leads to moksha.

Apart from all the messages and morals attributed to the great philosopher poet of the Mahabharata, I would say that the epic throws open to the man, in full unfettered freedom for his moksha (liberation), an opportunity to work, successively through faith, sacrifice and duty as Pandav brothers did. Karma and dharma are the two guiding principles, among many, running through the text of this great epic. Starting with the basic question that Arjuna posed as to why must we all kill and get killed just for a piece of land which he wouldn't have at any cost, there were other questions involved, which Arjuna did not know. In order to solve Arjuna's reservations, Lord Krishna makes him aware that his understanding of the world is limited. He then is obliged to show Arjuna his Virat Roop to remove his doubts, but before raises Arjuna to a state in which he is ready to undergo the mystic experience. This mystic experience which prevails upon Arjuna's human attachment is the Omnipotent Will of God or the Wheel of Karma in which the humans must stay moving gladly or grudgingly with their assigned `karmas' and be part of the one Universal Movement.

शान्ताकारं भुजगशायनं पद्मनाभं सुरेशं
विश्वाधारं गगनसदृशं मेघवर्णं शुभाङ्गम् ।
लक्ष्मीकान्तं कमलनयनं योगिभिर्ध्यानगम्यं
वन्दे विष्णुं भवभयहरं सर्वलोकैकनाथम् ॥

Rama Slaying the Demon-King Ravana

THE STORY OF RAMAYANA

The Family Tree
Descending through Surya, Manu and

Ikshvaku, and later

Important kings of the Dynasty:
    Bhagirath
    Raghu
    Harishchandra
    Sagar
    <u>Dashrath:</u>

By Kaushalya	By Kekai	By Sumitra
Rama	Bharat	Lakshman, Shatrugna

Sita - Wife of Rama

Janak - King of Janakpuri and father of Sita

Vishishtha - Family priest and guru

Celebrated senior saints of the realm:
Vishwamitra
Bhardwaja
Valmiki
Attri
Sharbhanga

Ravana - Demon king of Shri Lanka who stole Sita and
        invited war.
Vibhishna - Ravana's younger brother who broke away from

from Ravana.
Shurpnakha - Sister of Ravana

Hanumana - Rama's most loving devotee (bhakta) and most
   powerful general of his army.
Sugreeva - King of Kiskindhyapuri, and Rama's friend and
   ally.

In these prehistoric times, the whole world was persecuted and terrorized by the atrocities of king Ravana of Shri Lanka whose mercenary troops and other demonic powers under his command perpetrated inhuman wrongs on the people all over the land. Upon request from the people, gods, gandharvas, nags and kinners, led by Brahma, Vishnu, and Mahesh, approached the Lord God and apprised him of the situation, and reminded Him of his
pledge to help on such occasions. The Lord God while conceding the right of the persons to attain to any height through their deeds as Ravana did, told all the assembly that none however powerfully booned, could transgress the limits of dharma which is the law paramount and could not be disobeyed without punishment. Hence the Lord God agreed to send Rama on earth as his incarnation to help establish the rule of law and dharma.

Birth and Schooling of Rama & Brothers

King Dashratha of the Suryavanshi clan was ruling India with his capital at Ayodhya. He had three queens but no son for want of which he used to be worried as it could stop his family line. At the counselling of the royal priest Rishi Vishishta, he organized the Putra Kameshti Yajna in consequence of which his three queens got four sons: Kaushalya gave birth to Rama, the second queen Kekai had Bharat and two twins Lakshman and Shatrugna were born to the third queen

Sumitra. As they reached the school-going age, they were sent to the gurukula (boarding school) of Rishi Vishishta where they received education in Vedas, Shastras and all other branches of learning including warfare. All the brothers turned out to be full-grown warriors with qualities of head and heart, Rama excelling in all of them. On completing the long and arduous course of study, they returned home after receiving convocational benediction from their guru Vishishta and giving him gurudakshina promises to follow the path of dharma and service to the people selflessly.

Taraka Badh

By then the yogis and saints in the realm who were engaged in their spiritual and scientific pursuits got really sick of the day-to-day disturbances from the men of the rakshasha king Ravana who did not like Aryan people develop their material power to become superior to them. They all went to the leading most revered Rishi Vishwamitra for help. Through his yogic powers, the rishi knew that a real savior had taken birth as Rama in the house of king Dashratha of Ayodhya where he should go to borrow Rama so he could bring an end to that menace. Hence the rishi went to the king and asked for his two sons Rama and Lakshman. The king was reluctant at first to part with their two loving sons whom he thought too young to prevail upon the demons Taraka and her sons in whose jurisdiction lay the troubled spots. As refusal could have cost the king gravely at the hands of the displeased spiritual master, he finally let Rama and Lakshman go with the rishi trusting that godly powers of the rishi were their help and support.

Rama and Lakshman gladly accepted the challenge and eagerly awaited the confrontation with the woman demon Taraka and her sons Marich and Subahu and their hosts. Soon they came to fight but got killed one by one except Marich who fled away to save his life. Rishi Vishwamitra was very pleased at the task well done as there was peace and quiet all over.

Salvation of Ahalya

On the way they came across many religious places and important sites which the rishi carefully explained to Rama and Lakshman with full religious and spiritual significance. One of the sites seen was the Rock Ahalya where in long penance, Sati Ahalya lay awaiting the arrival of Lord Rama to liberate her of her guilt through deception played upon her by the treacherous Devraj Indra. Here the great rishi told the tragic story of a faithful innocent woman who was deceptively seduced by one great man and punished for no fault of her by another great man, her husband, none other but Rishi Gautam: Once in the early hours of the morning when Rishi Gautam was gone for a long walk, Indra who had been longing for rishi's extremely beautiful wife Ahalya, entered her house disguised as Rishi Gautama and seduced her pretending that he was Rishi Gautama. As Indra was getting out of her house, the rishi came upon the spot, recognized him in disguise and understood what had happened. Infuriated at her allowing Indra in the house, the rishi gave a curse to his wife turning her into a rock and desired her to stay buried until Rama on his journey to the forest would touch the rock with his foot and release her of the bondage. Rama, who was filled with pity and compassion for the innocent woman, immediately touched the rock with his foot and brought her to life and heaven. This is one of the many legendary acts of `patit pawan' bhagwan Rama.

Breaking of Shiva's Bow and Sita Svayambar

Upon receiving invitation from Raja Janak of Mithila to participate in the svayambar (wedding by choice) of her daughter Sita, Rishi Vishvamitra along with Rama and Lakshman, resumed their journey and reached Janakpuri where King Janak personally received them and made suitable arrangements for their stay. On the scheduled day of the swayambra, they went to witness the ceremony. The condition of the marriage was that whoever, among the assembled kings and princes, would successfully lift and wield the great bow of Shiva which was lying in the custody of the king, he would marry the most beautiful and meritorious Sita. All the kings and princes tried but failed to move the bow not to mention lifting it. At last on the suggestion of his guru Vishwamitra, Rama rose to wield the brow and broke it in the attempt to wield it to the amazement of all and the joy of king Janak and Sita who instantly garlanded him for her husband. This happy event was disturbed by the appearance of Bhagwan Parshurama who did not want that any one should tamper with the great bow of his deity Shankara. He now wanted to punish the person who had broken the bow. Rama humbly and respectfully resolved the problem by shooting a special arrow that Parsurama gave him to shoot in order to test his divinity.

Rama Exiled

Soon after returning home from marriage at Janakpuri, the king began thinking of his old age and retirement from the responsibilities of the government. Upon the advice of the royal priest Vishishta and the Chief Minister Arya Sumantra, he desired that his eldest son Rama be made the king. Since there was no doubt in anybody's mind about the ability of Rama to be an able successor to his father, there was rejoicing at the news all over the kindgom. A date for the coronation was announced and preparations in full swing were started at all levels. When all were happy and joyful at the coming event, the second queen Kekai became unhappy and disturbed on instigation from her maid servant Manthra who advised her to frustrate the design of the king as a result of which she was bound to be relegated to a place inferior to the mother of the new king. Burning from jealousy with her rival who would be the queen mother, she insisted on the king to fulfill her two promises that he had granted her for the help she had given the king in a battle with the asuras in which the king was seriously wounded. Well now the queen Kekai wanted the king to make good his promises by making her son Bharat the king of Ayodhya instead of Rama, and sending Rama to exile into the forests for fourteen years so that he would not be an obstacle in the rule by her son. So in the midst of the festivities, Kekai went into mourning, sent for the king immediately, and asked him to redeem her two promises then and there. While the king was shocked at the unreasonable demand of her queen, and begged her to desist from her wickedness, Rama at once agreed to go to the forest to fulfill the promise that his father had made to the queen. His wife Sita and younger brother Lakshaman would not stay behind and accompanied him. Hence all three departed for the forest against the wishes of all family members and the people of Ayodhya city.

Bhaarat Milap

Two younger brothers Bharat and Shatrugna who had since been out of the town returned home on receiving urgent message from the family guru and guide Rishi Vishishta. They were shocked and grief stricken to know that their father had died unable to bear the tragedy that had befallen the family. Bharat refused to take the throne which, he insisted, belonged to Rama; and promised that he would either bring Rama back or stay with him in the forest as long as it takes. After cremation of his father, he organized a royal procession and along with Guru Vishishta, the three mothers and other officials of the state proceeded toward the forest. He had a deeply emotional meeting with Rama and insisted him to return home, or allow him to stay with him in the forest. Rama was determined to fulfill the promise given by his father to queen Kekai and must keep it at all cost; but Bharat for his love of his elder brother Rama had taken a vow to take him back home. The matter became too complex to be solved easily, and was referred to Guru Vishishta and King Janak who also by then had arrived in the forest. As meeting after meeting failed to persuade Rama to return home, he was finally made agreeable to accept the crown on condition that Bharat would act only as his agent caretaker of the government until Rama returned home on completion of the fourteen years of exile. On returning to Ayodhya, Bharat renounced all palatial living and retired to a hermitage built outside the city from where he conducted the affairs of the state on behalf of his master Rama.

Rishi Attri-Anusuya, Rishi Sharbhanga, and Rishi Agastha

After Bharat left, Rama, Lakshman and Sita abandoned Chitrakoot to avoid interference from visitors since most people in the area had come to know of the place. They arrived at the ashram of Rishi Attri and his wife Anusuya who knew Rama, the divine, and his presence in the area. Sati Anusuya known to have gained spiritual powers by virtue of her service to her hussband spoke words of wisdom to Sita, gave her heavenly jewelry and garments and blessed her while Rishi Attri appreciated the task undertaken by Rama and familiarized Rama with the dangers ahead since the area south of them was in anarchy and was infested with Ravana's rakshashas and many notorious demons. He also advised Rama not to miss meeting Rishi Sharbhanga who had little time left on earth and was waiting only to meet Him. Rama, Lakshman and Sita took leave of the Rishi and his wife Anusuya and hurried toward the ashram of Rishi Sharbhanga appropriately dealing with rakshashas who tried to block their way. As soon as they entered the ashram of Rishi Sharbhanga, they found him talking with Devraj Indra who had come to personally take him to heaven for all the good deeds he had done. The rishi declined Indra's offer saying that as a karma yogi, he would go only at his own will and not necessarily in the heaven. Devraj Indra argued that since even as a human his full tenure on earth was over, he might as well take him away as he had come there any way. The rishi again refused to go saying that he had a more important visitor in Rama awaiting him on his ashram's doorsteps.

After Devraj Indra was sent away, the rishi received Rama, Sita and Lakshman and was happy to meet them saying that he had no more wish left to be on the earth. The rishi offered to give Rama all his spiritual powers which he had acquired all his life, but Rama gratefully refused to take them saying he would rather earn the merit with his own hard work (karmas) than through a free gift which would be tantamount to stealing. The rishi was happy at the expected answer and blessed them all in their task ahead. On taking leave of them, the rishi disappeared into the elements after cremating himself in the midair.

Upon leaving Sharbhanga rishi's ashram, they roamed around the forest killing rakshashas who came to attack them, and then arrived at Muni Agashta's ashram. Muni Agastha is fabled to help deva in their battle against the asuras, to stop the growth of Vindhyachal mountain which wanted to rise higher to block the sunlight going across; and he is known to have brought down River Caveri to the South from the heavens. He also was the one who developed Tamil language to make it one of the greatest languages. He was "the one who in order to keep the balance of knowledge at par between the North and the South went South from where all the learned people had gone to the North to witness Shankra's wedding." It is said that he was the one learned man in the South against all the learned men of the North; and lest the balance should tilt against the South, he never abandoned the South!" Such was the great Rishi Agastha who through his yogic powers was awaiting the arrival of Lord Rama and was pleased to see him arrive in his ashram. After giving Rama, Lakshman and Sita full hospitality, he gave Rama necessary wisdom and very unique and invincible arms - bows, arrows, including the Amodh Ban, and at the same time warned him of the dangers ahead which they had to meet as destined. He then bade them farewell.

Sharoopnakha And Khar Dooshan

They next moved to Dandak Ban on the bank of river Godvari where Lakshman built a hut for themselves; and they started living there encountering whatever problems came from rakshashas and utilizing their time in meditation and spiritual discussions. One day Shurpnakha, sister of Ravana, happened to visit that area and fell in love with the two handsome Aryan youths living there with a woman. Disguised as a bewitching beauty, she approached Rama with the proposal to marry her. On being refused by Rama as he was already married, she went to Lakshman who too declined her offer saying that he was only a servant of his master Rama and could not afford the luxury. Angrily she returned to Rama and tried to kill Sita so that Rama could marry her, but vigilant Lakshman stopped her from attacking Sita by cutting her nose. This incident sparked off a much more serious trouble than they perhaps anticipated in these unfriendly lands when there was just one year left for them to complete their fourteen years in the exile.

With her bleeding nose, Shurpnakha went running to the nearby military cantonment of their brothers Khar and Dushan who were enraged to see that the two Aryan youths had insulted their sister in that way. They immediately dispatched a force of soldiers and followed it personally. Both Khar and Dushan along with their army were killed by Rama alone; and Shurpnakha now in sheer shock and disappointment went straight to the court of Ravana in Lanka. Ravana was stunned and distressed at the news but at the same time inflamed to know that just two humans had dared to challenge the rakshasha king in that manner. He immediately began plans to punish the two Aryan youths especially enticed by the thought of grabbing the most beautiful Sita who, from Shurpnakha's description, `was fit only to be kept in the palace of his brother Ravana.'

Ravana Steals Sita

The legendary Ravana with ten heads and twenty arms symbolizing physical and intellectual power was the king of Sri Lanka. He was stronger than anyone in the then non-Aryan world. He was a sworn enemy of all peace loving people who hated his autocratic rule. A great devotee of Shankra, he had pleased him by great sacrifices and in return had received unique powers which had humbled the devatas. Enticed by the thought of making the beautiful Sita as his queen, he devised ways and means to attain his objective. Preferring cunning to direct confrontation in a battle with Rama, he ordered his uncle Marich to become a golden deer through his magic powers and tantalize Sita by grazing in front of her cottage so that, on Sita's request, Rama and Lakshman would get out of the cottage to chase him and give him an opportunity to steal her in their absence. Marich knew Rama's strength but agreed to play the game preferring to be killed by Rama, the divine, than by Ravana for disobeying his orders. So he went and started grazing in front of their cottage. On seeing the golden deer moving in front of her very eyes, Sita could not resist the temptation of possessing such a valuable thing. She immediately persuaded Rama to catch it for her pleasure. Lakshman tried to discourage Rama but Rama had to please Sita. After a hot chase, Rama killed the deer but was surprised to see him crying Lakshman for help in human voice. On hearing the cry for Lakshman's help, Sita got worried about Rama's safety and goaded Lakshman to go to his brother's help. Lakshman smelling some trickery tried to dismiss the cry saying that Rama was all powerful. On her being nasty, Lakshman left after drawing a magic line in front of the cottage instructing her not to cross it at any cost. After seeing Lakshman gone, Ravana appeared disguised as an old hungry yogi and called the occupant of the cottage for something to eat. On seeing the hungry old yogi begging for food at her doorstep, she immediately came out and even crossed the Lakshman Line (rekha) to give the food to the beggar. Ravana immediately caught hold of her, put her in his wayuyan (airplane) and began cruising on his journey to Lanka. Her wailing and crying for help was in vain. People, whether they be Rama or Sita, get lost, when they transgress the limits of normal behavior bewitched by the wicked golden deer or careless of the good Lakshman Line.

Jatayu, Sugreeva, and Bali

As Rama saw the dying deer turning Marich and Lakshman approaching him in the forest, he imagined that something wrong had happened to Sita. They rushed back to their cottage but found it empty. They then ran helter and skelter searching her around but in vain. Then, at a distance, they spotted Jatayu moaning in pain but holding on to his life so that on meeting Rama, he could tell him what had happened to Sita and his own failure to help, he being mortally wounded by Ravana. Rama was grateful to Jataya who was his father's friend. He then cremated him and proceeded further in search of Sita, but soon approached a blockade of huge arms of a handsome gana turned demon by the curse of a rishi. He was awaiting to be killed and cremated by Rama to regain his beautiful form as a gana. On cremation and returning to his human form, the gana, by his psychic powers, told that Ravana had carried Sita to the South, and Sugreeva, the king of banars living on the Rishimuk Parvat would be a great help to him. For further help in the matter they were directed to meet mata Shabri in Rishi Matang's Ashram, whom the rishi had told all about it before dying a short while ago. Soon they arrived at Rishi Matang's Ashram and met mata Shabri who gave Rama fruits after herself tasting them to be sweet. Rama ate them with love and regard showing that Rama loved all, high or low, equally. With directions given by Shabri, the two brothers proceeded toward Rishimuk Parvat, and on the way, were met by Hanumana who approached them disguised as a brahman trying to investigate if they were not the enemies of his master Sugreeva. After satisfactory mutual introductions, Hanumana took Rama and Lakshman to Sugreeva who was glad to find a strong ally in Rama to help him regain his wife and kingdom from his stronger older brother Bali. Both Rama and Sugreeva promised to help each other. Since Sugreeva's enemy Bali was close by, Rama offered to help him first. Evaluating their strategy one day when the two brothers were engaged in a deadly duel, Rama killed Bali with his arrow. The apparent unfairness of this act of Rama was justifiably explained that one who is unjust and one who had robbed his younger brother's wife could be killed even without due process.

Hanuman and Lanka Burning

After the death of Bali and with his wife returned to him, Sugreeva was crowned king of Kishkindhyapuri. On becoming the king, he was lost in revelry for awhile but was soon roused by prudent Hanumana and Jamwant on getting signal from Lakshman. He felt sorry for the delay but immediately gathered his ministers and trusted warriors to go in search for Sita. They sent the leading generals like Hanumana and Jamwant. They were informed that Ravana had hidden Sita in his capital in Lanka which was quite a distance away across the ocean. To cross the ocean and reach Lanka with an army seemed impossible; but before that they had to be sure that Sita was alive and was in Lanka city where Ravana lived. They then searched for someone physically strong, mentally alert, bestowed with spiritual powers and willing and devoted to the cause of Lord Rama who could locate Sita so that with suitable preparations Lanka could be invaded. As Hanumana was the person they found best qualified to undertake this mission, they returned to Sugreeva and Rama for permission and blessings for Hanumana to proceed to Lanka. Rama was happy to know that none but his very own Hanumana was going on that important mission. He gave him his ring as an identification and assurance to Sita that he was soon coming to emancipate her after destroying Ravana.

Travelling across the ocean on way to Lanka, many hurdles came in the way of Hanumana. Sursa demon with her huge open mouth wanted to devour him. But with the speed of wind, of which he was the personification, and dedication and daring, he dashed past all the problems and landed himself in Lanka sooner than he had thought. Unfamiliar with the topography of the city in the night time, he started making random checks so that after searching in vain in the palaces, he spotted a house with Rama written on it. It surprised him because he did not expect that in Landa there could a person devoted to Lord Rama. He entered the house, woke up the lone occupant Vibhishna, and after mutual introduction, asked him where he could locate Sitaji. Vibhishna promptly told him all about Sita's welfare and her located under a tree in Ashok Vatika, the famous royal garden of king Ravana. At once Hanumana arrived at the Ashok Vatika, stole himself into it and made himself seated on tree under which Sita was sitting meditating on Rama. Ravana had just returned after threatening to kill her and when the guards were preparing to retire for their nightly rest. At this time Hanumana got down and revealed himself to Sita and told her the purpose of his visit. On seeing Hanumana and Rama's ring which he gave her, she was thrilled and felt confident that all her woes would soon be over. As Hanumana's mission also included evaluating Ravana's strength for the upcoming war, he damaged his garden to be able to meet him, and battled with the guards, and even killed his son who came to apprehend him. The infuriated Ravana immediately sent his older son Indrajit to capture Hanumana, dead or alive. Promptly Indrajit arrived, and after a brief battle succeeded in arresting Hanumana with the help of his Brahma Astra. Hanumana respectfully got bound voluntarily in regard for Brahma. Hanumana was presented before Ravana and humiliated by all courtiers except the noble Vibhishana who counseled Ravana not to kill the messenger of the enemy but release him after light punishment. Ravana wanted to teach a good lesson to

Hanumana. Therefore, on suggestions from all, he agreed to the burning of Hanumana's long tail by wrapping layers of oily cloth around it. As soon as they set Hanumana's tail on fire, he torched it into the palace of Ravana and the important buildings of the city so that within a short time the whole city was ablaze. On burning Lanka thus, Hanumana returned to Sita mata for her blessings and then returned home.

Hanumana's return to Kiskindhyapuri with the discovery of Sitaji and burning of Lanka was an event of immense happiness and relief to Rama and Lakshman. It gave great joy and satisfaction to king Sugreeva and his court including the entire army and the anxiously awaiting general public. There was no doubt in anybody's mind that the next step would be to invade Lanka. The invasion seemed easy, but the crossing of the ocean seemed difficult. Meantime, Vibhishana, the younger brother of Ravana arrived after abandoning Ravana who had expelled him from his kingdom with insults. He suggested that a bridge be laid over the ocean; but before that the ocean himself should be asked to voluntarily become dry to enable the forces to march through. For three days and three nights the entire army led by king Sugreeva and his generals and Rama and Lakshman was waiting upon the sea god to make way for them until at last Rama took his bow and wielded his Agni Ban in order to dry the ocean by burning it. The terrified ocean appeared with folded hands and asked apologies for the delay in presenting himself. He then expressed his readiness to comply with Rama's wishes provided he would not let his prestige be diminished by getting dry as Rama himself is the upholder of the prestige of all. Rama would not embarrass the ocean, but asked him the alternative. The ocean suggested Rama to have a bridge built over him connecting Lanka with the help of the two brilliant engineers Nal and Neel, in Sugreeva's army, who were endowed with the power of floating big rocks and even hills on the water. Immediately, the task of building the bridge was assigned to Nal and Neel; and within a short time a bridge was built with thousands of banars joined together in carrying materials. As soon as the bridge was ready, Sugreeva ordered the banar forces to get across and make their cantonment at Subel Parvat on the coast of Lanka.

At Subel Parvat with permission from Rama, an emergency meeting of the high command was held to plan a strategy for the invasion. Before they did that a consensus was reached in which it was decided that Ravana should be approached once again to respectfully return Sitaji and avoid the impending bloodshed in which thousands would lose their lives. Hence Angad, son of Bali, was sent as an emissary in the court of Ravana who treated him no better than he had treated Hanumana. Angad showed him his prowess by challenging any one from his court to lift his foot which he fixed to the ground with full strength. When none could lift his foot, he warned Ravana that in Rama's forces there were thousands of warriors like him and there was no doubt that he would lose the war. Stubborn Ravana did not listen to any reason. Disappointed Angad returned to his cantonment.

War became a certainty. Orders were issued to the captains to stand firm on all fronts and move gradually toward the army of Ravana which, in the meantime, came marching on. Each column met its corresponding column to give it a pitched battle. Ravana was surrounded by several leading warriors who fought against him one by one, and was later challenged by Rama himself. Meantime Lakshman battled with Ravana's older son Indrajit who wounded him critically which worried Rama; but Lakshman was soon cured by a wonderdrug brought overnight by Hanumana from the Himalayas. As soon as he got up he prepared to battle with Indrajit again who had gone to please his favorite deity for invincible powers. He had to be pulled out in the midst of his yajna which would have made him invincible; and after a short battle was killed by Lakshman to the relief of Rama and the joy of all his forces. Ravana's younger brother Kumbhkaran now entered the war, but was soon killed by Rama leaving only Ravana in the battlefield.

Rama started by cutting Ravana's ten heads one by one, but they reappeared as soon as they were cut off which puzzled him for a while. But Vibhishna knew the secret of Ravana's invincibility. He advised Rama that Ravana had the nectar in his abdomen, which must be dried up with the karal ban. Rama did the same thing and killed Ravana instantaneously. The death of Ravana was hailed by all the people, including gods who came to congratulate Rama. Ravana's dead body was returned to his wife Mandodari for his last rites in which all the leading men participated from both sides.

Rama then sent Hanumana to Ashoka Vatika to respectfully bring Sitaji to the cantonment where after proper ceremonies, including the `Agnipreeksha' she joined him. As promised, Rama made Vibhishana the new king of Lanka and himself prepared to return home after giving blessings to all in Lanka. He and Sita returned in a wayuvan (airplane) along with Lakshman and Hanumana and took the same route by which they had come on the way meeting the saints and seers and the people who had been impatiently waiting for his return home in triumph.

After crossing Yamuna, Ganga, and meeting his old friend Nishadraj Guhu, he reached Ayodhya. Before entering the city, he sent Hanumana to inform Bharat of his arrival. Bharat was in a very bad state of health living like a hermit outside the city. He was anxious to meet Rama any minute but determined to die if he would delay his arrival any longer. In a moment Hanumana arrived and greeted him with the news of Rama's arrival. On hearing the news, Bharat was wild with joy, and in ecstatic frenzy, ran toward the spot where Rama was leaving the people to follow him in an excited unending stream. On meeting, Bharat prostrated at the feet of Rama and Sita, embraced Lakshamana and Hanumana and brought all of them home in full royal procession to the happiness of all the citizens. On taking over the reins of the kingdom from Bharat, Rama, true to his principles, rules his subjects with love and compassion for a long time. Of all the great rules in history, he is known to have given his people a rule of peace and happiness based on dharma popularly known as `Rama Rajya' where no one was unhappy.

MAHABHARATA

"THEY ARE ALREADY SLAIN BY ME;

YOU BE THE INSTRUMENT."

THE STORY OF THE MAHABHARATA

The Family Tree
Descending through Surya, Manu and Ikshvaku in an earlier yuga

Santanu

by Ganga: Bhisma

by Satyavati: Chitrangad - died unmarried
Vichitravirya - died childless
leaving two widows Ambika and Ambalika.

Through Ved Vyasa, Dhritrashtra, blind by birth, was born to Ambika, and Pandav was born to Ambalika.

To Dhritrashtra were born 100 sons, Duryodhana, the oldest, is the villain of the story.

To Pandav were born 5 sons: by Kunti - Yudhishtra, Bhima and Arjuna, and by Madari, Nakul and Sahadeva. Yudhishtra was the oldest.

1. Sage Ved Vyasa was Rishi Parashara's son from Satyavati when she was a maiden.

2. Vidur, the well-known statesman, was the son by sage Ved Vyasa and the maid servant of the widows of Vichitravirya.

3. Dronacharya son of Bhardwaja was the royal teacher of the princes and a great warrior.

4. Karan was the step brother of Pandavs by the sun god, born to

their mother Kunti as a maiden. He turned over to the Kauravs in order to challenge the best archer Arjuna, and for the honor and equal status given him by Duryodhana.

6. Draupadi, daughter of king Drupad and wife of the Pandavs.

7. Krishna, the God incarnate, leader of the Vrishni clan, and king of Dwarika.

Schooling of Princes

These were the times when king Santnu ruled Hastinapur. He had a son named Devavrata, later known as grand sire Bhisma, by his first wife Ganga. To ensure continuous succession to the throne, lest the only son might be lost prematurely, the king, in accordance with the custom, wanted to marry the beautiful Satyavati, the daughter of a fisherman. When the king made the proposal to the father of the girl, the fisherman readily agreed to marry his daughter to him on the condition that only his daughter's children would succeed to the throne and not the king's older son. The king rejected the proposal; but when young Devavrata came to know that he was in the way of his father's second marriage, he pledged that he would never take the throne of his father and would stay unmarried all his life so that he would beget no son who would thwart his pledge. He thus urged the fisherman to marry his daughter to his father. From his father's second marriage to Satyavati were born two sons Chitrangad and Vichitraviya. Chitrangad died unmarried, and Vichitravirya, though married to the princesses Ambika and Ambalika of Kashi, died childless. In order that the family line continues and the royal throne has a successor, the mother-in-law Satyavati requested the two widows to vicariously beget two sons by Rishi Ved Vyasa. Accordingly, Dhritrashtra was born to Ambika, and

Pandu to Ambalika. As ordained, their maid servant too got a son, named Vidur, by the Rishi. Because the older son Dhritrashtra was blind by birth, Pandu succeeded to the throne. Pandu proved to be a good king. He not only expanded his empire but brought peace and justice to the people. As ill luck would have it, he caused the death of Rishi Kindan who, while dying, cursed the king that he would die if he did not follow a certain rule of conduct. Therefore, Pandu soon died and was succeeded by his blind brother Dhritrashtra as the acting king until the family found an able heir to the throne.

Wax House and Draupadi Svayambar

Dhritrashtra was supposed to be a caretaker king, but he soon forgot his position and with the help of his brother-in-law Shakuni made plans so that, after his death, only his son Duryodhana, oldest of the one hundred he had, would become the king. Pandu had five sons named as Yudhishthira, Bhima, Arjuna, Nakul and Sahdeva of whom Yudhishthira was the oldest. Pandu sons always excelled Kauravas in education, archery and other games. So, they were the loving students of their famous guru Dronacharya and favorites of the elders and the people. The people of Hasthinapur loved and praised Pandu sons because they were good and kind, and wanted the noble Yudhishthira, the oldest of them, to be the crown prince. Duryodhana was naturally jealous of the Pandu sons; and, with the help of his friends and uncle Shakuni, he sought ways and means to kill Pandu sons. After a couple of local abortive plots to kill one or the other of his cousins, Duryodhana had a wax house built in a far off place of resort, and managed to send them there so that one night, when the house would be put on fire, they would be burnt alive. But the Pandavs escaped unhurt through their intelligence network after themselves burning the house a day earlier.

After escaping from the wax house, the Pandavs wandered

from place to place in search of friends and sympathizers. They came to know of Draupadi's swayambara (marriage by own choice) at the court of King Drupad of Panchal Pradesh. Disguised as brahmans, they participated in the swayambara; and to the amazement of all the assembled kings and princes, Arjuna fulfilled the condition of the swayambara when others had failed, and married princess Draupadi who later found out to her joy that the archer disguised as brahman was no other but the famous Arjuna. When Kunti, the mother of the Pandavs, was informed of `a prize' they had won, she blessed her sons and asked them to share the prize without knowing that the prize was the princess whom Arjuna had won. But the mother's decree, caused through spiritual prompting, was accepted by all the brothers; and Draupadi now became a common wife of all of them.

About the same time as Pandavs and Kauravs were born, there was born in a jail of the city of Mathura, about one hundred and fifty miles away, a baby boy named Krishna whose parents Vasudev and Devaki were imprisoned by Devaki's cruel brother Kans who had been foretold that he would be killed by a son of his sister. By keeping Devaki and her husband in jail, Kans maintained strict security over them and had all their children killed. But when Krishna, the God incarnate, was born, all the security staff went into deep slumber by divine power; and Krishna was secretly removed to the house of a respectable person Nanda in a nearby village across the river Yamuna. In this village Yashodha, the wife of Nanda, raised Krishna along with his older brother Balram. After proper education, Krishna now took leave of his adoptive parents so he could fulfill the task ahead of him. He first killed the cruel Kans and delivered the city of Mathura from his atrocities, and later moved along with all his clan to a new city of Dwarika of which he was crowned king and from where he directed the politics of India and guided his friends Pandavs in the civil war known as the Mahabharata. Pandavs were not only friends but close relatives of Krishna as Kunti, the mother of the three older Pandavs was the sister of Krishna's father. But Krishna's relationship with the Pandu brothers was unique in the sense that Krishna was personally bound to Arjuna in a spiritual attachment so that in the future civil war, he would guide the great archer Arjuna to victory.

Partition of Country

When the king at Hasthinapur learned that the Pandavs were alive and had also married princess Draupadi in the famous swayambara in which his sons had unsuccessfully participated, he was embarrassed; but he showed his outward happiness at the good news. The elders and the people of the city now desired that Pandavs be respectfully received back and Yudhishthira the oldest and ablest of all the princes of both families be declared as the crown prince against the wishes of the king and his friends and supporters. Fearing that Duryodhana, the king's oldest son, and his supporters would never accept Yudhishthira as their king, the grand sire Bhisma, Drona and others, at the suggestion of the king, agreed to partition the country and allot one half of the land to the Pandavs keeping the better part, including Hasthinapur, for the king and his sons. The portion thus given away was known as Khandavprastha which was a barren and hilly land; but the Pandavs, on inspiration from Lord Krishna and his brother Balram, worked hard and developed it into a beautiful productive country renaming its old city as Indraprastha to suit its splendor.

Pandavs' Ashvamedh Yajna

In course of time, the Pandavs evaluated their power and popularity to proclaim their suzerainty over all the kings in the land. Hence, they had an assembly of all the Indian kings and invited sages, seers and elders, especially Bhisma, Drona, and Vidura to formalize conferment on king Yudhishthira, the title of emperor, through the customary `Ashvamedh' yajna. In the assembly, Lord Krishna was proposed chairman, but king Shishupala tried to defeat the move by cursing Krishna in the open house to which all objected. Krishna tolerated Shishupala's tirade, but warned him that he could tolerate no more than one hundred curses exceeding which he was doomed to die at his hand. Shishupala went on cursing; and as soon as he crossed the one hundred limit, Lord Krishna moved to sever his head. The assembly was then called to order and Yudhishthira was declared emperor by popular vote to the dismay and disappointment of unhappy Kauravs.

Duryodhana was one of the royal guests. After the function was over, he was taken around to see the magnificent buildings and wonderful objects of art and architecture. On seeing the glory and splendor of the city, Duryodhana became jealous beyond description. Meantime, he was made fun of by Draupadi when, unable to differentiate between deceptive paintings and real water, he fell into a pool of water which added salt to his injury. He was, therefore, indignant beyond limit and he resolved to avenge the insult by Draupadi. He was immensely restless and wanted to see Pandavs lose their empire one way or another. Use of force was considered unwise at this time as Pandavs were known warriors. Besides, they had built connections like king Draupad through marriage and had family relations with other kings. His cunning uncle Shakuni made him a suggestion that if the king Yudhishthira, who was fond of gambling, could be lured into playing the game, they would cheat him into losing all his empire. This was thought to be a safe way of dislodging Pandavs of all their possessions. Duryodhana took no time to accept the proposal and promptly sent an invitation to Yudhishthira to play the game at Hasthinapura much against the wishes of the elders like Bhishma, Drona and Vidura.

Gambling and Loss of Empire

As expected, despite counseling and warnings from all concerned, Yudhishthira went to Hasthinapura with his brothers and was received with unusual love and respect. They got down to playing the game soon after arrival. Duryodhana persuaded the elders, and the pandavs to allow his master cheater Shakuni to play on his side `so that he could do the cheating for his victory.' And in accordance with the Kaurava's strategy and expectations, Yudhishthira started losing. He lost jewels, gold, silver, chariots, horses, cows, sheep, cities, villages, citizens of his kingdom, and lastly all his brothers who no longer were free persons. Yudhishthira lost all that he could conceive of. This is the compulsive nature of the vice - any vice that the poet Ved Vyasa tries to illustrate. Yet the addict is ever more ready to stake again and again in the vain hope of winning and recovering all that he had lost. Shakuni and his partners now reminded Yudhishthira that he still had his wife Draupadi to put at the stake. This offer, although viciously coming from the enemy, appeared like a boon to the addict Yudhishthira. So he immediately offered Draupadi, his next and last stake, in the wager disregarding all agitated protestations from the elders and the statesmen in the assembly as if he had lost all his senses. He did lose his senses as momentarily he lost her too, and shamelessly!

Draupadi Disgraced

Now came the most crucial moment of the whole drama when the winners, in order to prove to their humiliated adversaries, the extent of their power over them in the changed circumstances, had Draupadi dragged into the open court, and ordered that she be stripped off naked by Duryodhana's younger brother Dushashana. This indeed was the point on which the conscience of the whole Aryan society was invoked, as protection of the honor of the women folk was the cornerstone of the Aryan Hindu dharma (morals). Yet there was none to intervene, not even Bhisma and Drona, as all found themselves helpless to stop the lewd meanness the Kauravs, under inspiration from Shakuni and Karna, had planned. As Draupadi looked around for help and found none, she meditated on Lord Krishna, her only help; and He, true to His promise in the scriptures, frustrated the nefarious designs of the evildoers by endlessly extending her robes so that the pullers gave up in sheer fatigue to the scorn and shame from all around. As what in the beginning appeared to be a family fun had now turned into a sorry sordid episode, the elders in utter consternation compelled the king to cancel the despicable session, and asked the Pandavs to return home with all their possessions restored.

This sorry tale raised questions in the minds of all, particularly Draupadi, as to the right and authority of her husband to put her on the wager, especially when she was not his sole wife. He certainly had no right over her; but the poet tries to prove the compulsive nature of the addiction to the vice of gambling which deprives a person of the sense of right and wrong. This incident also illustrates the extent of degeneration in the society where respectable women could be publicly stripped off without shame or compunction, and even the responsible elders had no courage to oppose it for fear of losing their livelihoods.

But the worst had been perpetrated by Duryodhana and his brothers. Seeds of destruction were sown deep and deadly. The old king Dhritrashtra was worried that he had allowed such a grievous wrong to be done by his sons against his brother's sons Pandavs. His prime minister Vidur minced no words in condemnation and blamed thus: "....The victim of adverse fate will first become perverted, utterly losing his senses of right and wrong. Time, the all destroyer, does not take a club and break the head of a man but by destroying his judgment, makes him act madly to his own ruin. Your sons have grossly insulted Panchali and put themselves on the path of destruction."

After Yudhishthira and his brothers had returned, Duryodhana reproached his father for frustrating his plans as he never wanted him to return to Pandavs their lost possessions. As the devil would quote scriptures, he even quoted Brihaspati that every wrong means was right if it would destroy the enemy. He prevailed upon his father to invite the pandavs again for another gambling session which alone was the sure way to dislodge Pandavs of their rich possessions. On being persuaded by his loving son, the king sent another invitation. To Yudhishthira, like a kshatriya of those days, a challenge of whatever nature had to be accepted. Moreover, it was his nature to be drawn into gambling compulsively regardless of earlier victory or defeat. A smoker likes the company of the smokers; an alcoholic must go by the liquor shop; and persons fond of carnal pleasures do not usually miss frequenting the red areas as far as possible. This is the dictate of nature formed over years of addiction. Moreover the invitation could not have been refused, even if they had wanted to because an invitation coming from their uncle king Dhritrashtra, was an order which they were duty bound to accept knowing full well its implications as, by this time, they had known the designs of even the king whom they still revered in the traditional manner.

Another Game of Gambling and Pandavs Exiled

The Pandavs returned again to play another game of dice, this time with the stake that the loser would go with his brothers into an exile in the forest for thirteen years of which the thirteenth year would be spent incognito. If in the thirteenth year, they were recognized, they would go again into the exile for another thirteen years. Again, Yudhishthira lost the game against the deceitful master gambler Shakuni, who played on Duryodhana's side. Thus the Pandavs were bound to go to exile as per the terms of the game. With thousands to sympathize but none to help, they bowed before the inevitable and proceeded to the forest - all five of them accompanied by queen Draupadi.

Yudhishthira knew what had happened to them as this was foretold to him by sage Ved Vyasa at the time of his Ashvamedha Rajna. The sage had said that much of sorrow and suffering was in store for them for thirteen years and portents indicated the destruction of the kuru race as it was destined and none could avert it.

He advised Yudhishthira to be steadfast in righteousness. Hence, Pandavs accepted the exile as preordained and began making plans for their new life in the forest for the next thirteen years. They wandered place to place, and met friends and well-wishers who came to see them from all over the country. They were visited by several important saints to advise them on religion and morals. Lord Krishna came to apologize to Draupadi for not being able to come in person at the time of her need and vowed: "....I shall help the Pandavs in every way ... The heavens may fall, the Himalayas may split in twain, the earth may crumble or the bountless sea may dry up - but, I tell you verily, my words shall stand..." Balram, Krishna's older brother, argued that there was no logic or pleasure for him in taking sides as in both the camps, he had his dear ones and disciples. Some of the notable personalities they met in the course of their wanderings were sages Lomasa, Agastya, Markandeya Durvasa, and Hanumana. All these rishis counseled Pandavs on morals and methods of righteous living. Hanumana disguised as an old brahman met Bhima, and advised him to hold on to truth whatever be the consequence. One day when, upon Duryodhana's misbehavior with a gandharva girl in the forest, he was apprehended by them along with his friends, Pandavs were obliged to defend their very enemies Kauravs because Yudhishthira wouldn't want their own bretheren, however bad, to be humiliated by strangers, as it would have disgraced the fair name of the house of Kurus. In doing so, he established the rule that, as against outsiders, they were unitedly one hundred and five, not just one hundred.

Incognitos in Viratnagar

As the twelfth year ended and the Pandavs were supposed to live in disguise for the thirteenth year, as per the contract, they took leave of their retinue and retired to a secluded spot in a forest to plan where and how they should spend the next twelve months. Disguised differently, they came to the court of king Virata in search of jobs. Yudhishthira who looked like a learned saintly person was retained by the king as his counselor. Bhima was appointed cook while Arjuna, dressed as eunuch in the name of Brahannala, was hired to teach dancing and music to princess Uttra and the ladies of the court. Nakul was assigned the care of horses, and Sahadeva was placed in charge of the cows and the bulls. The princess Draupadi became the maid servant of queen Sudeshna.

The Pandavs had hardly settled in their new jobs when there arose a serious problem. The queen's brother Keechaka who was the commander-in-chief of the king's army fell in love with Draupadi and wanted to marry her by force. He even misbehaved with Draupadi one day. Draupadi complained about this to Bhima who promised to kill him. Lest their identity be known, he disguised himself as Draupadi, lured Keechaka into one of the rooms in the palace and killed him.

By now the Kauravs were trailing behind the Pandavs through their intelligence network to discover them so that, according to the condition, they could be sent into exile for another thirteen years. They instigated their friend king of Trigarta to invade the king of Matsya so that Virata would be obliged to help the latter and he could win only, as per their calculations, if the Pandavs would come to his assistance. In this way, Duryodhana thought, they could surely find out the whereabouts of the Pandavs. As the battle raged and the Pandavs joined the fighting on behalf of king Virata and defeated the Kaurav forces including Duryodhana himself and all his generals like Karna, Bhisma, and Drona, their identity was disclosed. But this disclosure came a day after the last day of the thirteenth year so the Pandavs were not obliged to stay in the hiding as they were then free men. This fact was recognized by the elders like Bhisma, Dronacharya, and Kripacharya, but rejected by Duryodhana and his group.

Pandavs then left king Virata and settled in Upaplavya from where they sent emissaries to summon their friends and relatives with their forces to mobilize a suitable army to fight the Kauravs, which appeared to be the only alternative left, should the Kauravs failed to listen to reason. Some of those offered to fight on their side were Yuyudhana, Virata, Drupada, Dhrishtaketu, Kuntibhoj, Uttamauja, Satyaki and the kings of the Kasis and the Sibis. To more important kings and personalities, the Pandavs thought of going in person. Thus, Arjuna went to Dwarika, to seek the help of Krishna, where he found Duryodhana already present for the same purpose. Lord Krishna split up his help into two parts: one was his entire army known as Naraini Sena, the other was he in person, unarmed and pledged not to wield any weapon. On Duryodhana's choosing Krishna's army in preference to him unwilling to take up arms, Arjuna's wish was fulfilled as he could not ask for more than his friend by his side even unwilling to wield weapons. Arjuna requested Krishna to be his charioteer as, it is in this way only that he could be with him in the war all the time. Balram, though did not quite appreciate Yudhishthira's cause since he was only to blame for his troubles in consequence of his addiction to gambling, refused to take Duryodhana's side either because with relations on both sides, he wanted to stay out of the war. Salya, the maternal uncle of the Pandavs Nakul and Sahadev went to Kauravs as Pandavs failed to give him a proper reception. But mighty Satyaki joined the Pandav forces thus bringing the total Pandav forces to seven divisions as against eleven of the Kauravs

Final Bid for Peace by Krishna

Before the Pandavs would declare war, Krishna suggested to Pandavs that they should try all means for a peaceful settlement. First they sent king Draupada's brahman messenger to seek a just solution. Then they received the minister Sanjay from Dhritrashtra supplicating peace but without promise to return their kingdom. Yudhishthira even told Sanjay that the Pandavs would be satisfied with only five villages as the price for saving the whole Kuru race from destruction in the war. But Duryodhana stubbornly refused to agree to return any portion of their kingdom. Lord Krishna made a last minute dash to Hasthinapur to persuade Duryodhana to avoid a bloody war, but got a defiant refusal from him saying that he would not give even a needlepoint of the territory without war. At one point when Krishna upbraided Duryodhana for his intransigence, he ordered that Krishna be captured in the court itself; but Krishna ridiculed his stupidity by momentarily showing his virat swaroop (cosmic form). The war now became an imminent certainty as Krishna returned to Upaplavya deeply hurt and disappointed.

Kurukshetra (Dharamkshetra), the traditionally sacred place (incidentally, the birth place of this author) was mutually approved to be the battlefield for the great civil war known as the Mahabharata. Both sides stood arrayed in battle formations with commanders ready to give orders. Commander-in-chief of the Kuru forces was grand sire Bhisma while the Pandav army was commanded by Dhristdyumna, the younger son of king Drupad, who was burning with rage to avenge the wrong done to his sister Draupadi by Duryodhana and to his father by Dronacharya who, being a revered teacher of the Pandavs, had chosen to fight against them.

Arjuna Refuses to Fight and is Lectured

Now as both sides blew their respective conches (war bugles) to begin the fighting, Arjuna refused to fight. He put his mighty bow aside. His nerve fails him as he is overtaken by attachment and love of life. He reasons to Lord Krishna thus: he will not slay his own kith and kin and his elders particularly Bhisma and the beloved teacher Dronacharya for the sake of all the three worlds much less the little kingdom. He would better be a beggar than be an instrument in the slaughter of his race. "To convince him that he must fight, Krishna is not content merely to use arguments already familiar to him - his caste duty as a warrior, for instance; he sees fit rather to reveal to him the structure of the universe as it really is and in which Arjuna is merely a pawn moved by the hand of an all-powerful God whose will no man or god can resist or thwart." Arjuna was shown the celestial but awfully cosmic personality of Him, the God incarnate. So he was stricken with unspeakable wonderment unable to say anything. He, therefore, bade him to return to his previous loving human form, and promised to do all that he would want him to do now when all his doubts were resolved. And presently the Lord God returned to his human form, ready to do Arjuna's bidding as his charioteer in the war.

The Great War

After Krishna's great Lecture and their salutations to the elders, Pandavs started the war which began with full fury and lasted for eighteen days killing all the Kauravs and both the armies except guru Dronacharya's son Ashwatthama who had a boon for dying at will. Even though it was a dharma yudha - the war of righteousness and both sides had laid down the rules of the fighting, both sides broke them without compunction: As the commander-in-chief of the Kuru army, Bhisma was unfairly armed with the boon of dying at will, king Drupad's son Shikhandi (formerly a princess of Kashi) had the boon to avenge her humiliation by Bhisma who had wrongfully refused to marry her in a previous life. Hence, Bhisma's invincibility was countered by Shikhandi backed by Arjuna's arrows felling him as the first casualty of the war. To this Kauravs reacted in a more mean and treacherous manner when almost all the leading warriors of the Kuru army by violating the one-against-one rule, defeated, disarmed, and mercilessly butchered Abhimanya, the teenager son of Arjuna. This infuriated Pandavs to such a degree that even the sanest person of them all, Yudhishthira, succummed to lying for victory if lying was not as sinful as the sins Kauravs had been perpetrating against them. Krishna knew that Pandavs could not kill the great teacher Dronacharya in a fair fight. Reacting to the earlier deceitful killing of Abhimanyu by the Kauravs, the Pandavs were justified to hatch some sort of a scheme to remove him from the battlefield: Upon Krishna's suggestion that if Dronacharya was convinced that his son Ashvatthama was killed, he would be nerve broken and lay down his arms in grief and make himself an easy target, the Pandavs reluctantly agreed as they had no other choice. Therefore, when the announcement of Ashvatthama's death was made by Bhima, and falsely confirmed to Drona by the truthful Yudhishthira, Drona behaved as expected, and was beheaded by Drishtdyumna.

Even the God incarnate Krishna himself was half way into breaking his vow not to wield arms as, swayed by anger, he twice rushed for his arms against the Kauravs in sheer attachment for his friends Pandavs. And he himself justified the tit for tat which lasted till the end of the war when, upon seeing Duryodhana mortally wounded by Bhima, though unfairly, the sole survivor of the Kauravs Ashwatthama, in order to avenge the death of his father Dronacharya, killed Dristdyumna and the five sons of the Pandavs by sneaking into their camp at night only to find later that the persons he killed were not five

Pandu brothers, but their five sons. When Pandavs came to know that Ashwatthama was responsible for that ghastly act, they gave him a hot chase and seized him hidden in the Rishi Ved Vyasa's ashram in the Himalaya.

As Ashwatthama had the boon of dying at will, Pandavs could not kill him. Yet in self defense, he shot his all destructive arrow (Pashupat missile) to kill the Pandavs, which was opposed by Arjuna shooting his own equally deadly missile. Since both sides seemed to hang, and mass destruction from the missiles on both sides would produce no solution, Rishi Ved Vyasa, who was watching the drama of the war by his spiritual powers, stepped in. He counseled both parties to withdraw their weapons of mass destruction which had to stop at some point or they would annihilate the whole mankind. At Krishna's suggestion Arjuna withdrew his missile promptly, but Ashwatthama was incapable of controlling his. So he was cursed by the rishi to live a miserable life as long as he lived.

BANDE KRISHNAM JAGADGURU